SpringerBriefs in Operations Research

SpringerBriefs present concise summaries of cutting-edge research and practical applications across a wide spectrum of fields. Featuring compact volumes of 50 to 125 pages, the series covers a range of content from professional to academic. Typical topics might include:

- A timely report of state-of-the art analytical techniques
- A bridge between new research results, as published in journal articles, and a contextual literature review
- A snapshot of a hot or emerging topic
- An in-depth case study or clinical example
- A presentation of core concepts that students must understand in order to make independent contributions

SpringerBriefs in Operations Research showcase emerging theory, empirical research, and practical application in the various areas of operations research, management science, and related fields, from a global author community. Briefs are characterized by fast, global electronic dissemination, standard publishing contracts, standardized manuscript preparation and formatting guidelines, and expedited production schedules.

More information about this series at http://www.springer.com/series/11467

Enrique Mu • Milagros Pereyra-Rojas

Practical Decision Making using Super Decisions v3

An Introduction to The Analytic Hierarchy Process

Springer

Enrique Mu
Carlow University
Pittsburgh, PA, USA

Milagros Pereyra-Rojas
University of Pittsburgh
Pittsburgh, PA, USA

ISSN 2195-0482 ISSN 2195-0504 (electronic)
SpringerBriefs in Operations Research
ISBN 978-3-319-68368-3 ISBN 978-3-319-68369-0 (eBook)
https://doi.org/10.1007/978-3-319-68369-0

Library of Congress Control Number: 2017955836

Printed on acid-free paper

This Springer imprint is published by Springer Nature
The registered company is Springer International Publishing AG
The registered company address is: Gewerbestrasse 11, 6330 Cham, Switzerland

This book is dedicated to the memory of Thomas L. Saaty (1926–2017). He gave the world a better way to make decisions and inspired a whole generation of scholars. Thank you, Tom!

Pittsburgh, August 25, 2017

Preface

The field of AHP decision-making is in continuous development. Most recently, the Creative Decisions Foundation has launched its new Super Decisions v3. This version constitutes a drastic departure from the previous versions. Creative Decisions Foundation may either maintain both current software versions (v2 and v3) in operation, so practitioners may take advantage of the different strengths of these two versions, or may decide to gradually phase out Super Decisions v2; however, which path will be taken is still unknown. While Super Decisions v2 has attractive graphical features, Super Decisions v3 offers an easy interface, in particular for ratings models. This convinced us of the need to write a book, which would allow practitioners and scholars to learn, use, and teach AHP using Super Decisions v3. While the theoretical part of this book is basically the same as in our previous book *Practical Decision Making: An Introduction to the Analytic Hierarchy Process (AHP) Using Super Decisions v2*, the practical part is taught using the newly released Super Decisions v3.

Pittsburgh, PA, USA
June 2017

Enrique Mu
Milagros Pereyra-Rojas

Acknowledgments

This book would not have been possible without the assistance of Dr. Elena Rokou, chief research officer at the Creative Decisions Foundation and developer of the new Super Decision v3. She generously assisted the authors with the laborious task of getting familiar with a new software version during its beta test. Also, Ms. Rozann Saaty, vice-president of the Creative Decisions Foundation, was very encouraging—as usual—with our initiative and, finally, Dr. Thomas Saaty, who warmly welcomed us into his classes where we were able to follow up on the use of the new software version in his course. He never ceases to inspire us.

Audience for This Book

Since the landmark publication of *Decision Making for Leaders* by Thomas L. Saaty in 1980, there have been several books on the topic. Some of them deal with the theory of the analytic hierarchy process (AHP), and others discuss its applications. The question is whether a new book on AHP is needed and why. The answer is based on our own experience as academic and practitioner of the AHP methodology.

First, AHP appeared as an intuitive and mathematically simple methodology in the field of multi-criteria decision-making in operations research (OR). Because of this, most AHP books assume the reader has basic OR mathematical background. Even books that claim to be extremely simple to understand usually demand from the reader "basic linear algebra and familiarity with vectors" as a prerequisite. Truthfully, these books are very simple to understand if you have the requested mathematical background. However, the problem starts when we try to teach AHP to decision-makers outside the OR field. AHP simplicity suggests that decision-makers from all disciplines can take advantage of the methodology if they can learn it without having to struggle with the mathematical jargon, no matter how simple it can be for an OR professional.

Teaching AHP fundamentals and applications to non-OR students requires a different approach from the one offered by traditional books. Similarly, when explaining and teaching the AHP method to corporate executives, it becomes clear that these professionals are in the best position to take advantage of using the AHP method, but at the same time, they lack the time or interest to learn the math behind it. An approach that could provide them with a quick understanding of the method and, most importantly, learn it well enough to use it in their business decisions is needed.

This book aims to fill in this need. It provides a quick and intuitive understanding of the methodology using spreadsheet examples and explains in a step-by-step fashion how to use the method using *Super Decisions*, a freely available software developed by the *Creative Decisions Foundation*. The high-school level of math is used in this book, and we have avoided using sophisticated terms to make the procedure easy to understand. This book is based on a 15-year experience practicing and teaching AHP to executives and non-OR students and is based on class notes developed for this purpose over time. Because of this, we are also indebted to our AHP students for inspiring us to write this book.

Contents

How to Use This Book

This book provides a very simple, practical, and quick introduction to the theory and practice of the analytic hierarchy process and has been defined in a modular way for practical purposes.

If you are interested in the **theory and practice of AHP using Super Decisions v3**, read this book in the sequence provided in the Table of Contents; that is, from Chap. 1 to Chap. 10 where the basic level is constituted by Chaps. 1–3, intermediate by Chaps. 4–7, and advanced by Chaps. 8–10. You may also benefit from reading appendices A and B although these are optional and software independent.

If you would like to get familiar with the fundamentals of the **AHP theory only**, without learning any software package, you may just want to read Chaps. 1, 2, 5, 7, 8, 9, and 10. Should you want to further your knowledge of the mathematical fundamentals of the theory, you may also want to read Appendix B.

If you are already familiar with the AHP theory and want to use this book as a **practical introduction to the Super Decisions v3**, you may jump ahead to Chap. 3 (developing models) followed by Chap. 4 (adding sub-criteria) and Chap. 6 (ratings model). Appendix A is convenient since it is related to the practice of AHP.

As you can see, we are trying to honor our commitment of making this book a practical introduction to AHP decision-making and suitable for the diverse needs of our readers.

Introduction

Human beings are required to make decisions at individual and collective levels. Initially, the decision-making process was studied as a rational process of analyzing a problem and seeking solutions; however, in recent years, it has become clear that human beings are far from making decisions in a rational way, either as an individual or as part of a group.

Psychological studies have found cognitive anomalies or biases experienced by human beings when making decisions (Kahneman 2011). These cognitive biases and the increasing complexity of modern problems make it extremely important to adopt a methodology for making straightforward (easy to use and understand), effective (making consistent decisions according to our criteria and interests), and safe (proven methodology) decisions.

The analytic hierarchy process (AHP) meets all these requirements, and since its appearance in 1980, it has been adopted and used by a large number of institutions all over the world. For these reasons, this is the method that will be presented here for practical decision-making.

There are several books dealing with AHP theory and practice. This book is different in the sense that it intends to provide you with a practical introduction of AHP. In other words, upon reading this book, you will be able to start using AHP in practical applications.

Reference

Kahneman, D. (2011). *Thinking fast and slow*. New York: Farrar, Straus and Giroux.

Part I
Basics

Chapter 1
The Need for Another Decision-Making Methodology

Abstract Henry Mintzberg defined three types of management roles: interpersonal, informational, and decisional (1989). Interpersonal refers to the ability of the manager of being a figure head, motivational, and a liaison with the public (e.g., Steve Jobs at Apple). Informational refers to the manager's role as information broker and disseminator. Decisional refers to the power and ability of making decisions.

Henry Mintzberg defined three types of management roles: interpersonal, informational, and decisional (1989). Interpersonal refers to the ability of the manager of being a figure head, motivational, and a liaison with the public (e.g., Steve Jobs at Apple). Informational refers to the manager's role as information broker and disseminator. Decisional refers to the power and ability of making decisions.

While Mintzberg argued that different managers have different role abilities, he highlights that managers have the authority and power of committing their organizations to courses of actions that will lead to successful or funnest outcomes. Based on this, being an effective decision-maker is a fundamental skill for managers and leaders alike. In the end, it is the right and wrong decisions that will make the firm succeed or fail. This is quite true not just at the organizational level but also at the individual level.

1.1 The Need for Decision-Making Methodologies

The most popular model of decision-making at the individual level was proposed by Simon (1960) and defines decision-making as a process comprising the steps of: intelligence, design, selection, and implementation. The stage of *intelligence* is associated with the question: What is the decision we face? The *design* stage allows you to propose alternatives and criteria to evaluate them while the *selection* stage consists of applying the proposed criteria to choose the best alternative(s) to the problem. Finally, the last step is to *implement* the chosen alternative.

This model, as well as other similar models, assumes individuals are rational information processors that seek to maximize the benefits of their decisions (economic behavior); however, these assumptions have been strongly questioned in

E. Mu, M. Pereyra-Rojas, *Practical Decision Making using Super Decisions v3*, SpringerBriefs in Operations Research, https://doi.org/10.1007/978-3-319-68369-0_1

recent years (Camerer, 1994). Experiments in cognitive psychology have shown that individuals are easy victims of a series of cognitive biases such as the phenomenon of framing (changing the way a decision is framed—e.g., as a win or a loss—makes individuals change their opinions), anchoring (the individual's decision is influenced by what piece of information is shown first), and many other cognitive biases (Kahneman, 2011).

For example, if two investment projects are presented to a group of people, one where there is the probability of losing 20% of the investment and another in which there is 80% chance of making a profit; people prefer to invest in the second project, although both have the same risk (20% probability of losing and 80% winning). This is an example of the phenomenon of preference based on the frame of reference (framing). In general, humans feel more inclined to proposals that are presented in positive terms (e.g., earnings) rather than those that are presented in negative terms (e.g., losses).

In other studies, it has been found that if a group of individuals is asked to estimate the following product: $2 \times 3 \times 4 \times 5 \times 6 \times 7 \times 8 \times 9$ and another group composed of individuals of similar age, education, etc. are asked to estimate the product $9 \times 8 \times 7 \times 6 \times 5 \times 4 \times 3 \times 2$; the first group estimates systematically lower results than the second group. This is because people are influenced by the first numbers shown. This phenomenon is called anchoring; somehow the person's estimate is defined or "anchored" by what is shown first.

In other words, these studies prove that human beings are not cold and calculating information processors. The fact that individuals may choose alternatives independently of their economic benefits does not speak well of the individuals in their role as *homo economicus.*[1]

Unfortunately, these cognitive biases do not simply occur as isolated cases, but their constant influence on financial, political, social, and professional decisions has been demonstrated (Piattelli-Palmerini, 1994). For example, in 1982, McNeil, Sox, and Tversky subjected a select group of doctors in the United States to a test. Using real clinical data, these researchers showed that doctors were so prone to make mistakes based on the decision's frame of reference (framing error) as anyone else. If doctors were informed that there was a 7% expected mortality for people undergoing a certain surgery, they hesitated to recommend it; if on the other hand, they were told there was a 93% chance of survival to the operation, they were more inclined to recommend the surgery to their patients.

If this happens with medical professionals, what can you expect from the rest of us? While there are several famous cases of fatally flawed individual decisions, decisions at group level have not fared much better. At the group level, disastrous decisions such as the invasion of the Bay of Pigs under President Kennedy or the madness of investments in Internet companies have been also attributed to problems associated with decision-making cognitive biases. Undoubtedly, there is a need for decision-making methodologies that can help to minimize biases and increase the likelihood of making effective decisions.

[1]An amusing discussion of how people can make irrational decisions is provided by Dan Ariely in *Predictably Irrational: The Hidden Forces that Shape Our Decisions.* Harper Perennial.

One of the reasons for the interest in working in groups in modern organizations is precisely the possibility of minimizing cognitive biases and to obtain group participation's synergy; however, this has not proven to be the ultimate solution to the problems of decision-making. Organizational psychology has shown that as part of a group, individuals are also exposed to a number of problems that hinder group decision-making (Forsyth, 2013). Among these group cognitive biases, we can mention *groupthinking*, consisting of the individual's desire not to act (or decide) different than what seems the consensus in the group (Janis, 1972). Another group bias is caused by *power unbalance* which makes the members of the group with less power and influence try not to antagonize those of greater power in the group, etc.

1.2 Decision-Making Methodologies

Perhaps the best known method for decision-making, described by Benjamin Franklin in a letter to Joseph Priestley, is the called Pros and Cons list. In this method, the problem is clearly stated, alternative possible solutions are proposed, and the pros and cons of each are established. Then, according to the importance of each PRO/CON factor and how it can be traded with the others (for example, the benefit/satisfaction provided by a specific PRO may be canceled out by the cost/pain of two specific CONS), the best alternative is determined based on the net result of this PRO/CON trading.

This method is, despite its limitations, a great improvement over simply following one's intuition to make a decision. The advantages of this method (and the majority of decision-making methods in general) are that it allows: first, the structuring of a problem that at first glance may not seem possible to structure; and second, sharing the decision criteria with others to get more ideas and opinions. The above approach works well for simple problems but has the disadvantage of not being able to accurately quantify the relative importance of each factor to be traded. Moreover, the process is complicated when the number of alternatives and factors becomes very large. A better method is needed.

There are several methods of decision-making but most require specific training in areas such as economics, operations research, and probability. However, what is needed is a methodology that can be applied in a more natural way by decision-makers.

The analytic hierarchy process (AHP) developed by Professor Thomas Saaty in 1980 allows for structuring the decision hierarchically (to reduce its complexity) and shows relationships between objectives (or criteria) and the possible alternatives. Perhaps the biggest advantage of this method is that it allows the inclusion of intangibles such as experience, subjective preferences, and intuition, in a logical and structured way.

The popularity of this method has increased since its implementation as computer software in the mid-1980s and the development of group decision support systems such as *Decision Lens* (Decision Lens, 2015). The analytic hierarchy process has been used by institutions in over 50 countries worldwide and the *Super Decisions* software (Super Decisions, 2015), available free of charge from the *Creative Decisions Foundation*, allows a user-friendly application of the AHP methodology (Creative Decisions Foundation, 2015). The *Creative Decisions Foundation* and *Super Decision* software websites provide information on the latest developments and news of the method and its applications.

1.3 Conclusion

The Analytic Hierarchy Process (AHP) has been widely discussed and used since its official appearance (Saaty, 2012). While there have been several discussions related to some aspects of AHP theory and practice [see, for example, Brunnelli (2015)], these objections have been addressed to the point that AHP constitutes one of the most widely used multi-criteria decision-making methods worldwide due to its intuitiveness and mathematical rigor. From its origins in the academia and the government to its use in Fortune 500 firms, it has moved to part of the essential tools of modern managers and leaders.

References

Brunnelli, M. (2015). *Introduction to the analytic hierarchy process*. Cham: Springer.

Camerer, C. (1994). In J. H. Hagel & A. Roth (Eds.), *Handbook of experimental psychology*. Princeton: Princeton University Press.

Creative Decisions Foundation. (2015). *Creative Decision Foundation*. Retrieved from http://www.creativedecisions.net

Decision Lens. (2015). *Decision Lens*. Retrieved from http://www.decisionlens.com

Forsyth, D. R. (2013). *Group dynamics* (6th ed.). Belmont: Wadsworth Publishing.

Janis, I. L. (1972). *Victims of group thinking*. Boston: Houghton-Mifflin.

Kahneman, D. (2011). *Thinking fast and slow*. New York: Farrar, Straus and Giroux.

Mintzberg, H. (1989). *Mintzberg on management: Inside our strange world of organizations*. New York: The Free Press.

Piattelli-Palmerini, M. (1994). *Inevitable illusions: How mistakes of reason rule our minds*. New York: Wiley.

Saaty, T. L. (2012). *Decision making for leaders: The analytic hierarchy process for decisions in a complex world* (3rd Rev. ed.). Pittsburgh: RWS Publications.

Simon, H. A. (1960). *The new science of management decision*. New York: Harper & Row.

Super Decisions. (2015). *Super Decisions*. Retrieved from http://www.superdecisions.com

Chapter 2
Understanding the Analytic Hierarchy Process

Abstract In this chapter, we will explain the fundamentals of the Analytic Hierarchy Process. The reader is referred to the original Saaty's (2012) discussion of AHP or to Brunnelli's (2015) for a theoretical introduction to the method. In this book, AHP concepts will be explained from a practical point of view, using examples for greater clarity.

In this chapter, we will explain the fundamentals of the Analytic Hierarchy Process. The reader is referred to the original Saaty's (2012) discussion of AHP or to Brunnelli's (2015) for a theoretical introduction to the method. In this book, AHP concepts will be explained from a practical point of view, using examples for greater clarity.

To explain this method we will use a simple example[1]: Our goal is to purchase a new car. Our purchase is based on different criteria such as cost, comfort, and safety (the reader can think of many more but we will use only three for illustration purposes). We could evaluate several alternatives but let us assume that we have only two: Car 1 and Car 2. To analyze the decision of purchasing a car using the analytic hierarchy process we should follow the next steps:

1. Develop a model for the decision: Break down the decision into a hierarchy of goals, criteria, and alternatives.
2. Derive priorities (weights) for the criteria: The importance of criteria is compared pairwise with respect to the desired goal to derive their weights. We then check the consistency of judgments; that is, a review of the judgments is done in order to ensure a reasonable level of consistency in terms of proportionality and transitivity.
3. Derive local priorities (preferences) for the alternatives: Derive priorities or the alternatives with respect to each criterion separately (following a similar process

[1] For this chapter, it is recommended that the reader follows the calculations of this example using a spreadsheet.

Electronic Supplementary Material The online version of this chapter (https://doi.org/10.1007/978-3-319-68369-0_2) contains supplementary material, which is available to authorized users.

E. Mu, M. Pereyra-Rojas, *Practical Decision Making using Super Decisions v3*,
SpringerBriefs in Operations Research, https://doi.org/10.1007/978-3-319-68369-0_2

as in the previous step, i.e., compare the alternatives pairwise with respect to each criterion). Check and adjust the consistency as required.
4. Derive overall priorities (model synthesis): All alternative priorities obtained are combined as a weighted sum—to take into account the weight of each criterion—to establish the overall priorities of the alternatives. The alternative with the highest overall priority constitutes the best choice.
5. Perform sensitivity analysis: A study of how changes in the weights of the criteria could affect the result is done to understand the rationale behind the obtained results.
6. Making a final decision: Based on the synthesis results and sensitivity analysis, a decision can be made.

At this point, the reader may feel a little intimidated by terms such as judgments, priorities, pairwise comparison, and consistency; however, the following discussion will clarify these topics.

2.1 Developing a Model

The first step in an AHP analysis is to build a hierarchy for the decision. This is also called decision modeling and it simply consists of building a hierarchy to analyze the decision.

The analytic hierarchy process (AHP) structures the problem as a hierarchy. Figure 2.1 shows the hierarchy proposed for our example. Note that the first level of the hierarchy is our goal; in our example, buying a car. The second level in the hierarchy is constituted by the criteria we will use to decide the purchase. In our

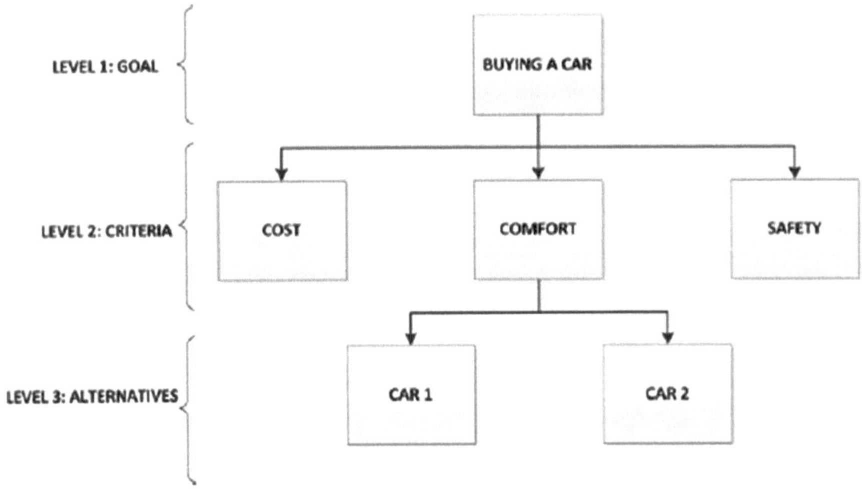

Fig. 2.1 Decision hierarchy for buying a car

Table 2.1 Saaty's pairwise comparison scale

Verbal judgment	Numeric value
Extremely important	9
	8
Very strongly more important	7
	6
Strongly more important	5
	4
Moderately more important	3
	2
Equally important	1

Table 2.2 Pairwise comparison matrix of criteria for buying a car

Buying a car	Cost	Comfort	Safety
Cost			
Comfort			
Safety			

example, we have mentioned three criteria: cost, comfort, and safety. The third level consists of the available alternatives.[2] In this case: Car 1 and Car 2.

The advantages of this hierarchical decomposition are clear. By structuring the problem in this way it is possible to better understand the decision to be achieved, the criteria to be used, and the alternatives to be evaluated. This step is crucial and this is where, in more complex problems, it is possible to request the participation of experts to ensure that all criteria and possible alternatives have been considered. Also note that in complex problems it may be necessary to include additional levels in the hierarchy such as sub-criteria.

2.2 Deriving Priorities (Weights) for the Criteria

Not all the criteria will have the same importance. Therefore, the second step in the AHP process is to derive the relative priorities (weights) for the criteria. It is called relative because the obtained criteria priorities are measured with respect to each other as we will see in the following discussion.

It is clear that when buying a car (as in other decisions), not all criteria are equally important in a given time. For example, a student may give more importance to the cost factor rather than to comfort and safety, while a parent may give more importance to the safety factor rather than to the others. Clearly, the importance or weight of each criterion will be different and because of this, we first are required to derive by pairwise comparisons the relative priority of each criterion with respect to each

[2] Each criterion, alternative, and the goal are collectively referred as model elements.

Table 2.3 Pairwise comparison matrix with intensity judgments

Buying a car	Cost	Comfort	Safety
Cost	1	7	3
Comfort	1/7	1	1/3
Safety	1/3	3	1

Table 2.4 Column addition

Buying a car	Cost	Comfort	Safety
Cost	1.000	7.000	3.000
Comfort	0.143	1.000	0.333
Safety	0.333	3.000	1.000
Sum	1.476	11.000	4.333

Table 2.5 Normalized matrix

Buying a car	Cost	Comfort	Safety
Cost	0.677	0.636	0.692
Comfort	0.097	0.091	0.077
Safety	0.226	0.273	0.231

of the others using a numerical scale for comparison developed by Saaty (2012) as shown in Table 2.1.[3]

To perform the pairwise comparison you need to create a comparison matrix of the criteria involved in the decision, as shown in Table 2.2.

Cells in comparison matrices will have a value from the numeric scale shown in Table 2.1 to reflect our relative preference (also called intensity judgment or simply judgment) in each of the compared pairs. For example, if we consider that cost is very *strongly more important* than the comfort factor, the cost-comfort comparison cell (i.e., the intersection of the row "cost" and column "comfort") will contain the value 7 as shown in Table 2.3. Mathematically this means that the ratio of the importance of cost versus the importance of comfort is seven (cost/comfort = 7). Because of this, the opposite comparison, the importance of comfort relative to the importance of cost, will yield the reciprocal of this value (comfort/cost = 1/7) as shown in the comfort-cost cell in the comparison matrix in Table 2.3. The rationale is intuitively obvious. For example, if in daily life we say that an apple A is twice as big as apple B (A/B = 2), this implies that apple B is half the size of apple A (B/A = 1/2). Similarly, if we consider that cost is *moderately more important* than safety (cost/safety = 3), we will enter 3 in the cost-safety cell (using the scale from Table 2.1) and the safety-cost cell will contain the reciprocal 1/3 (safety/cost = 1/3). Finally, if we feel that safety is *moderately more important* than comfort, the safety-comfort

[3] In this figure, the intermediate values 2, 4, 6, and 8 are used to address situations of uncertainty. For example, when the decision-maker is in doubt whether to rate a pairwise comparison as "moderately more important (3)" or "strongly more important (5)," a possible solution is to rate it as "From moderately to strongly more important"; that is, a 4.

Table 2.6 Calculation of priorities: row averages

Buying a car	Cost	Comfort	Safety	Priority
Cost	0.677	0.636	0.692	**0.669**
Comfort	0.097	0.091	0.077	**0.088**
Safety	0.226	0.273	0.231	**0.243**

Table 2.7 Presentation of results: original judgments and priorities

Buying a car	Cost	Comfort	Safety	Priority
Cost	1.000	7.000	3.000	**0.669**
Comfort	0.143	1.000	0.333	**0.088**
Safety	0.333	3.000	1.000	**0.243**

Table 2.8 Consistency indices for a randomly generated matrix

n	3	4	5	6
RI	0.58	0.9	1.12	1.24

cell will contain the value 3 and the comfortsafety cell will have the reciprocal 1/3. Once all these judgments are entered in the pairwise comparison matrix (Table 2.2), we obtain the results shown in Table 2.3.

Note in the comparison matrix of Table 2.3 that when the importance of a criterion is compared with itself; for example, cost versus cost, comfort versus comfort, or safety versus safety; the input value is 1 which corresponds to the intensity of equal importance in the scale of Table 2.1. This is intuitively sound because the ratio of the importance of a given criterion with respect to the importance of itself will always be equal.

At this stage, you can see one of the great advantages of the analytic hierarchy process: its natural simplicity. Regardless of how many factors are involved in making the decision, the AHP method only requires to compare a pair of elements at any time; something that, because of our pair anatomy (e.g., two hands), we have done for centuries. Another important advantage is that it allows the inclusion of tangible variables (e.g., cost) as well as intangible ones (e.g., comfort) as criteria in the decision. The comparison matrix (Table 2.3) shows the pairwise relative priorities for the criteria. We now need to calculate the overall priorities or weights of the criteria. There are two methods available for this purpose: the exact and the approximate.

Although we will not show the *exact method* in detail here, the general idea is very simple. Raise the comparison matrix to powers (e.g., raise the matrix to the power of two, raise the resulting matrix to the power of two again, and so forth) a few times until all the columns become identical. This is called the limit matrix. At this point, any of the matrix columns constitutes the desired set of priorities. This calculation can be done in a spreadsheet but it is currently done very easily using AHP-based software packages.

Table 2.9 Prioritization results

Buying a car	Cost	Comfort	Safety	Priority
Cost	1.000	7.000	3.000	0.669
Comfort	0.143	1.000	0.333	0.088
Safety	0.333	3.000	1.000	0.243

Table 2.10 Priorities as factors

Buying a car	Cost	Comfort	Safety
Criteria weights ->	*0.669*	*0.088*	*0.243*
Cost	1.000	7.000	3.000
Comfort	0.143	1.000	0.333
Safety	0.333	3.000	1.000

As we aim to explain roughly the elements of the AHP method, we will rather use the *approximate method* in our example due to its simplicity. However, keep in mind that this method provides a valid approximation to the overall weights only when the comparison matrix has a very low inconsistency.[4]

The *approximate method* requires the normalization of the comparison matrix; i.e., add the values in each column (Table 2.4).

Next, divide each cell by the total of the column (Table 2.5). The normalized matrix is shown in Table 2.5.

From this normalized matrix, we obtain the overall or final priorities (Table 2.8) by simply calculating the average value of each row (e.g., for the cost row: 0.677 + 0.636 + 0.692)/3 = 0.669).

Although there is no standardized way of presenting the results, showing the comparison matrix with the original judgments (Table 2.4) along with the calculated priorities (obtained in Table 2.6) is a useful way to see the judgments and priorities at the same time, as it can be seen in Table 2.7.

According to the results in Table 2.7, it is clear that—for this example—we give more importance to the cost criterion (0.669), followed by safety (0.243). The comfort factor has a minimum weight (0.088) in our purchasing decision. Another important observation is that the pairwise comparison of criteria, through questions such as to purchase your car, what is more important: cost or comfort?, allows us to derive, based on our preferences, the final priorities or weights for the criteria. That is, the priorities are not assigned arbitrarily but are derived based on our judgments and preferences. These priorities have mathematical validity, as measurement values derived from a ratio scale, and have also an intuitive interpretation. From Table 2.7 we can interpret that cost has 66.9% of the overall importance of the criteria, followed by safety with 24.3% and comfort (8.8%), respectively.

[4] Inconsistency will be explained later in our discussion.

Table 2.11 Calculation of weighted columns

Buying a car	Cost	Comfort	Safety
Cost	0.669	0.617	0.729
Comfort	0.096	0.088	0.081
Safety	0.223	0.265	0.243

Table 2.12 Calculation of weighted sum

Buying a car	Cost	Comfort	Safety	Weighted sum
Cost	0.669	0.617	0.729	2.015
Comfort	0.096	0.088	0.081	0.265
Safety	0.223	0.265	0.243	0.731

2.3 Consistency

Once judgments have been entered, it is necessary to check that they are consistent. The idea of consistency is best illustrated in the following example: If you prefer an apple twice as much than a pear and a pear twice as much than an orange, how much would you prefer an apple with respect to an orange? The mathematically consistent answer is 4. Similarly, in a comparison matrix criteria, if we provide a value of 2 to the first criterion over the second and assign a value of 3 to the second criterion with respect to the third one, the value of preference of the first criterion with respect to the third one should be $2 \times 3 = 6$. However, if the decision-maker has assigned a value such as 4, 5, or 7, there would be a certain level of inconsistency in the matrix of judgments. Some inconsistency is expected and allowed in AHP analysis.

Since the numeric values are derived from the subjective preferences of individuals, it is impossible to avoid some inconsistencies in the final matrix of judgments. The question is how much inconsistency is acceptable. For this purpose, AHP calculates a consistency ratio (CR) comparing the consistency index (CI) of the matrix in question (the one with our judgments) versus the consistency index of a random-like matrix (RI). A random matrix is one where the judgments have been entered randomly and therefore it is expected to be highly inconsistent. More specifically, RI is the average CI of 500 randomly filled in matrices. Saaty (2012) provides the calculated RI value for matrices of different sizes as shown in Table 2.8.

In AHP, the consistency ratio is defined as CR where CR = CI/RI. Saaty (2012) has shown that a consistency ratio (CR) of 0.10 or less is acceptable to continue the AHP analysis. If the consistency ratio is greater than 0.10, it is necessary to revise the judgments to locate the cause of the inconsistency and correct it.

Since the calculation of the consistency ratio is easily performed by computer programs, we limit ourselves here to producing an estimate of this value as follows:

Table 2.13 Calculation of λ_{max}

Weighted sum	Priority	
2.015/	0.669 =	3.014
0.265/	0.088 =	3.002
0.731/	0.243 =	3.005
	Total	9.021
	Divide total by 3 to obtain Lambda$_{max}$ =	3.007

Table 2.14 Comparison with respect to cost

Cost	Car 1	Car 2
Car 1	1.000	7.000
Car 2	0.143	1.000
Sum	1.143	8.000

(a) Start with the matrix showing the judgment comparisons and derived priorities (Table 2.7) which is reprinted for convenience in Table 2.9.
(b) Use the priorities as factors (weights) for each column as shown in Table 2.10.
(c) Multiply each value in the first column of the comparison matrix in Table 2.10 by the first criterion priority (i.e., $1.000 \times 0.669 = 0.669$; $0.143 \times 0.669 = 0.096$; $0.333 \times 0.669 = 0.223$) as shown in the first column of Table 2.11; multiply each value in the second column of the second criterion priority; continue this process for all the columns of the comparison matrix (in our example, we have three columns). Table 2.11 shows the resulting matrix after this process has been completed.
(d) Add the values in each row to obtain a set of values called weighted sum as shown in Table 2.12.
(e) Divide the elements of the weighted sum vector (obtained in the previous step) by the corresponding priority of each criterion as shown in Table 2.13. Calculate the average of the values from the previous step; this value is called λ_{max}.

$$\lambda_{max} = (3.014 + 3.002 + 3.005)/3 = 3.007.$$

(f) Now we need to calculate the consistency index (CI) as follows:

$$CI = (\lambda_{max} - n)/(n-1)$$

where n is the number of compared elements (in our example, $n = 3$). Therefore,

$$\mathrm{CI} = (\lambda_{max} - n)/(n-1) = (3.007 - 3)/(3-1) = \mathbf{0.004}$$

(g) Now we can calculate the consistency ratio, defined as:

$$\mathrm{CR} = \mathrm{CI} / \mathrm{RI}$$

Therefore,

$$\mathrm{CR} = \mathrm{CI} / \mathrm{RI} = 0.004 / 0.58 = \mathbf{0.006}$$

CI is the consistency index calculated in the previous step with a value of 0.004. RI is the consistency index of a randomly generated comparison matrix and is available to the public in tables (Table 2.8). In other words, RI is the consistency index that would be obtained if the assigned judgment values were totally random. It is possible to show (this is beyond the scope of this book) that the value of RI depends on the number of items (n) that are being compared (see expected values shown in Table 2.8). It can be seen that for $n = 3$, RI = 0.58. Using these values for CI and RI, it can be calculated that

$$\mathrm{CR} = 0.004 / 0.58 = 0.006$$

Since this value of 0.006 for the proportion of inconsistency CR is less than 0.10, we can assume that our judgments matrix is reasonably consistent so we may continue the process of decision-making using AHP.

2.4 Deriving Local Priorities (Preferences) for the Alternatives

Our third step consists of deriving the relative priorities (preferences) of the alternatives with respect to each criterion. In other words, what are the priorities of the alternatives with respect to cost, comfort, and safety, respectively? Since these priorities are valid only with respect to each specific criterion, they are called local priorities to differentiate them from the overall priorities to be calculated later.

As indicated, we need to determine the priorities of the alternatives with respect to each of the criteria. For this purpose, we do a pairwise comparison (using the numeric scale from Table 2.1) of all the alternatives, with respect to each criterion, included in the decision-making model. In a model with two alternatives, it is required to make only one comparison (Alternative 1 with Alternative 2) for each criterion; a model with three alternatives would require to make three comparisons (Alternative 1 with Alternative 2, Alternative 2 with Alternative 3, and Alternative 1 with alternative 3) for each criterion; and so on. There will be as many alternative comparison matrices as there are criteria.

In our example, we only have two alternatives: Car 1 and Car 2 and we have three criteria. This means that there will be three comparison matrices corresponding to the following three comparisons:

With respect to the cost criterion: Compare Car 1 with Car 2.

With respect to the comfort criterion: Compare Car 1 with Car 2.

Table 2.15 Preference with respect to cost

Cost	Car 1	Car 2	Priority
Car 1	0.875	0.875	0.0875
Car 2	0.125	0.125	0.125

Table 2.16 Results with respect to cost

Cost	Car 1	Car 2	Priority
Car 1	1.000	7.000	0.875
Car 2	0.143	1.000	0.125

Table 2.17 Comparison with respect to comfort

Comfort	Car 1	Car 2
Car 1	1.000	0.200
Car 2	5.000	1.000
Sum	6.000	1.200

Table 2.18 Preference with respect to comfort

Comfort	Car 1	Car 2	Priority
Car 1	0.167	0.167	0.167
Car 2	0.833	0.833	0.833

With respect to the safety criterion: Compare Car 1 with Car 2.

We can do these comparisons through a series of questions as shown below with sample answers.

Comparison Question 1: With respect to the cost criterion, which alternative is preferable: Car 1 or Car 2?

For our example, let us assume that we prefer *very strongly* (using the scale in Table 2.1) the Car 1 over the Car 2. This means that in the Car 1–Car 2 cell (i.e., the cell intersected by the row "Car 1" and the column "Car 2") of our comparison matrix regarding cost alternatives (Table 2.14), we assign a value of 7 (value assigned using the scale from Table 2.1) to reflect our preference Similarly, we assign the reciprocal reverse 1/7 in the Car 2–Car 1 cell in the table.

By normalizing the matrix and averaging the rows we obtain the priorities (or preferences) for each of the alternatives (Table 2.15) with respect to cost.

Because these priorities apply only to the cost criterion, they are called *local priorities* with respect to cost. The results are summarized for convenience as shown in Table 2.16.

Comparison Question 2: With respect to the comfort criterion, which alternative is preferable: Car 1 or Car 2?

Assume that Car 2 is *strongly preferred* over the Car 1; that is, we assign a value of 5 (using scale from Table 2.1) in the cell Car 2–Car 1 in our comparison matrix regarding comfort alternatives and the reciprocal reverse 1/5 in the Car 1–Car 2 cell (see Table 2.17).

Table 2.19 Results with respect to comfort

Comfort	Car 1	Car 2	Priority
Car 1	1.000	0.200	0.167
Car 2	5.000	1.000	0.833

Table 2.20 Comparison with respect to safety

Safety	Car 1	Car 2
Car 1	1.000	0.111
Car 2	9.000	1.000
Sum	10.000	1.111

Table 2.21 Preferences with respect to safety

Safety	Car 1	Car 2	Priority
Car 1	0.100	0.100	0.100
Car 2	0.900	0.900	0.900

Table 2.22 Results with respect to safety

Safety	Car 1	Car 2	Priority
Car 1	1.000	0.111	0.100
Car 2	9.000	1.000	0.900

By normalizing the matrix and averaging the rows we obtain the local priorities (or preferences) for each one of the alternatives (Table 2.17) with respect to comfort. See Table 2.18.

The results are summarized in Table 2.19.

Comparison Question 3: With respect to the safety criterion, which alternative is preferable: Car 1 or Car 2?

For our example, let us say the Car 2 is extremely preferable to Car 1 with respect to this criterion. These judgments are entered numerically (using scale from Table 2.1) in the respective cells in Table 2.20.

By normalizing the matrix and averaging the rows we obtain the local priorities (or preferences) for each one of the alternatives (Table 2.21) with regard to safety.

The results are summarized in Table 2.22.

Notice that having only two alternatives to compare with respect to each criterion simplifies the calculations with respect to consistency. When there are only two elements to compare (in our example, Car 1 and Car 2), the respective comparison matrices (Tables 2.14, 2.17, and 2.20) will always be consistent (CR = 0). However, consistency must be checked if the number of elements pairwise compared is 3 or more.

We can summarize the results of this step by indicating that if our only criterion were cost, Car 1 would be our best option (priority = 0.875 in Table 2.16); if our

Table 2.23 Local priorities (or preferences) of the alternatives with respect to each criterion

Alternatives	Cost	Comfort	Safety
Car 1	0.875	0.167	0.100
Car 2	0.125	0.833	0.900

Table 2.24 Local priorities table as a base

	Cost	Comfort	Safety
Car 1	0.875	0.167	0.100
Car 2	0.125	0.833	0.900

Table 2.25 Preparation for weighing of priorities

	Cost	Comfort	Safety
Criteria weights ->	*0.669*	*0.088*	*0.243*
Car 1	0.875	0.167	0.100
Car 2	0.125	0.833	0.900

Table 2.26 Calculation of overall priorities

	Cost	Comfort	Safety	Overall priority
Criteria weights ->	*0.669*	*0.088*	*0.243*	
Car 1	0.585	0.015	0.024	0.624
Car 2	0.084	0.074	0.219	0.376

only criterion were comfort, our best bet would be the Car 2 (0.833 priority in Table 2.19) and finally, if our sole purchasing criteria were safety, our best option would be the Car 2 (0.900 priority in Table 2.22). As previously indicated, the priorities (preferences) of the alternatives, with respect to each criterion, are called local priorities (or preferences). The summary of the local priorities for each alternative is shown in Table 2.23.

2.5 Derive Overall Priorities (Model Synthesis)

Up to this point we have obtained local priorities which indicate the preferred alternative with respect to each criterion. In this fourth step, we need to calculate the overall priority (also called final priority)[5] for each alternative, that is, priorities that take into account not only our preference of alternatives for each criterion but also the fact that each criterion has a different weight. Given that we are using all the values provided in the model, this step is called model synthesis.

We start the calculation of the overall priority using the local priority of each alternative as the starting point (Table 2.23, also repeated for convenience as Table 2.24).

[5] It is customary to refer to overall (also called general or final) priorities of the alternatives when they are calculated with respect to the whole model, that is, after the synthesis process.

Table 2.27 Synthesis of the model

	Cost	Comfort	Safety	Overall priority
Criteria Weights ->	*0.669*	*0.088*	*0.243*	
Car 1	0.875	0.167	0.100	0.624
Car 2	0.125	0.833	0.900	0.376

Next, we need to take into consideration the weights of each criterion (from 2.8) and for this purpose they are inserted in the table as shown in Table 2.25.

For example, the cost criterion has a priority (or weight) of 0.669 and the Car 1 has a local priority (or preference) of 0.875 relative to cost; therefore, the weighted priority, with respect to cost, of the Car 1 is: 0.669 × 0.875 = 0.585. A similar calculation is necessary to obtain the Car 1 weighted priorities with respect to comfort and safety criteria. The resulting matrix is shown in Table 2.26. Finally, the overall priority of the Car 1 is obtained by adding these results along the row. This procedure is repeated for each of the alternatives being evaluated. The overall priorities of the alternatives are shown in the rightmost column of Table 2.26.

The calculations for each alternative are shown below and the results are presented in Table 2.27 following the convention of showing the local priorities (cells) and the weights for each criterion (at the top of each column). This process is called the model synthesis (see Table 2.27).

In other words

$$\text{Overall Priority of the}\,car\,1: 0.875\times 0.669 + 0.167\times 0.088 + 0.100\times 0.243 = 0.624$$
$$\text{Overall Priority of the}\,car\,2: 0.125\times 0.669 + 0.833\times 0.088 + 0.900\times 0.243 = 0.376$$

Now we can list the alternatives ordered by their overall priority or preference as follows:

Alternatives	Overall priority
1. ***Car 1***	**0.624**
2. *Car 2*	0.376

In other words, given the importance (or weight) of each buying criteria (cost, comfort, and safety), the Car 1 is preferable (overall priority = 0.624) compared to the Car 2 (overall priority = 0.376).

2.6 Sensitivity Analysis

The overall priorities will be heavily influenced by the weights given to the respective criteria. It is useful to perform a "what-if" analysis to see how the final results would have changed if the weights of the criteria would have been different. This process is called sensitivity analysis and constitutes the fifth step in our AHP methodology. Sensitivity analysis allows us to understand how robust is our original

Table 2.28 Original scenario—synthesis of the model

	Cost	Comfort	Safety	Overall priority
Criteria weights ->	*0.669*	*0.088*	*0.243*	
Car 1	0.875	0.167	0.100	0.624
Car 2	0.125	0.833	0.900	0.376

Table 2.29 Scenario—all criteria have the same weight

	Cost	Comfort	Safety	Overall priority
Criteria Weights ->	*0.333*	*0.333*	*0.333*	
Car 1	0.875	0.167	0.100	0.380
Car 2	0.125	0.833	0.900	0.619

Table 2.30 Third scenario: cost weight leading to equal preferences of the alternatives

	Cost	Comfort	Safety	Overall priority
Criteria weights	*0.500*	*0.250*	*0.250*	
Car 1	0.875	0.167	0.100	0.504
Car 2	0.125	0.833	0.900	0.496

decision and what are the drivers (i.e., which criteria influenced the original results). This is an important part of the process and, in general, no final decision should be made without performing sensitivity analysis.

Note that in our example (Table 2.27), the cost is of great importance (priority 0.669) and given that the Car 1 has a high local priority (0.875) for this single criterion, undoubtedly this influences the final result favorably for the Car 1. The questions that we can ask ourselves at this stage are: What would be the best alternative if we change the importance of the criteria? What if we give the same importance to all the criteria? And, what if we give more importance to safety or we consider it to be as important as the cost? and so on.

To perform a sensitivity analysis, it is necessary to make changes to the weights of the criterion and see how they change the overall priorities of the alternatives. To exemplify this we will analyze the following scenarios: (a) when all the criteria have the same weight and (b) what weight is needed for the cost criterion to lead to a tie in the overall priorities of the alternatives? (This is a logical question since we know cost is very important in the original analysis and Car 1 scores very high in this criterion causing Car 1 to be the best preference.) Table 2.28 is the original model synthesis (Table 2.27) where the most preferable option is the Car 1 (0.624).

Table 2.29 shows the case where all 3 criteria have the same weight (0.333). In this second scenario, the final choice no longer has the Car 1 but the Car 2 (0.619) as the best option. This is because the Car 2 wins in all criteria except for cost. By lowering the weight of cost (from 0.669 in the original scenario to 0.333 in the second stage), its cost disadvantage is not as noticeable.

This also suggests that the alternatives switch preferences when cost weighs in the range of 0.333–0.669. To calculate the break-even point we can try different weights for the cost and find that when the cost weighs approximately 0.5 of the overall criterion importance, the Car 1 and the Car 2 have the same preference for practical purposes. That is, both alternatives are equally preferred as shown in Table 2.30.

2.7 Making a Final Decision

Once the above steps have been completed, it is now possible to make a decision. This constitutes the last step in our AHP analysis. For this, it is necessary to compare the overall priorities obtained and whether the differences are large enough to make a clear choice. It is also necessary to analyze the results of the sensitivity analysis (Tables 2.28, 2.29, and 2.30). From this analysis, we can express our final recommendation as follows: If the importance of the cost is more than 50% of the overall importance of the criteria in the decision, the best alternative is the Car 1 (Table 2.28); however, if the importance of cost is much less than 50%, the Car 2 is the best decision (from Tables 2.29 and 2.30).

2.8 Conclusion

It is important to note that, contrary to the common belief, the system does not determine the decision we should make, rather, the results should be interpreted as a blueprint of preference and alternatives based on the level of importance obtained for the different criteria taking into consideration our comparative judgments. In other words, the AHP methodology allows us to determine which alternative is the most consistent with our criteria and the level of importance that we give them (Videos 2.1, 2.2, 2.3 and 2.4).

Although AHP calculations can be done using electronic spreadsheets, the appearance of software packages such as Expert Choice (2015) in the late eighties and Super Decisions (2015) and Decision Lens (2015) later on has made AHP mathematical calculations very easy to deal with. A survey of current AHP software packages is beyond the scope of this book. However, the reader is referred to Ishizaka and Nemery (2013) for a partial survey of AHP software packages.

References

Brunnelli, M. (2015). *Introduction to the analytic hierarchy process*. Cham: Springer.
Decision Lens. (2015). *Decision Lens*. Retrieved from: http://www.decisionlens.com
Expert Choice. (2015). *Expert Choice*. Retrieved from: http://www.expertchoice.com

Ishizaka, A., & Nemery, P. (2013). *Multi-criteria decision analysis: Methods and software*. West Sussex, UK: Wiley.
Saaty, T. L. (2012). *Decision making for leaders: The analytic hierarchy process for decisions in a complex world* (3rd revised ed.). Pittsburgh: RWS Publications.
Super Decisions. (2015). *Super Decisions*. Retrieved from: http://www.superdecisions.com

Suggested Reading[6]

Developing a Model https://mix.office.com/watch/17icbrnswidq0.
Deriving Priorities (weights) for the Criteria https://mix.office.com/watch/4odxenri07nm.
Deriving Local Priorities (preferences) for the Alternatives https://mix.office.com/watch/1idaxl30c6o5o.
Deriving Overall Priorities https://mix.office.com/watch/ztkx3ea8lki8.

[6]These videos are the same as those provided in the supplementary material section but the links below are provided as alternative links and for redundancy purposes.

Chapter 3
Building AHP Models Using Super Decisions v3

Abstract Super Decisions v3 is the latest version of the software package developed for the analysis, synthesis, and justification of complex decisions based on the analytic hierarchy process (AHP) methodology.

The purpose of this section is not to teach all the possible uses of Super Decisions—which can be used not only for AHP but also for its generalization ANP (analytic network process)—but rather to illustrate the fundamentals of the software when applied to AHP analysis in decision-making. For this purpose we use Super Decisions v3, the most recent version developed by the Creative Decisions Foundation (2017). Readers are encouraged to review all Super Decisions v3 documentation available in the Super Decisions website (Super Decisions, 2017).

For illustration purposes, we will use a classic AHP example: the purchase of a car. Our purchase will be based on four criteria (or objectives): Cost, comfort, aesthetics, and safety. We can evaluate several alternatives but for our purposes let's assume we have three: Car 1, Car 2, and Car 3.

The reader will note that we have four criteria and three alternatives in this example. Having four criteria and three alternatives means that we need to complete five comparison matrices: Comparing criteria with respect to the goal (one matrix) and comparing alternatives against each of the four criteria (four matrices). Also, we need to ensure that the consistency ratio (CR) is less than 0.10 in all the comparison matrices. This level of complexity will allow us to appreciate the advantage of using Super Decisions. As the number of criteria and alternatives increases, the required number of pairwise comparisons also increases. If the decision-maker were using a spreadsheet, the complexity of the consistency calculation and related adjustments would increase drastically. Here is where Super Decisions becomes extremely useful by allowing the user to work with a large number of criteria and alternatives while hiding the complexity of the AHP calculations.

The steps required to reach a decision using Super Decisions are basically the same as in the AHP method. These steps are summarized as follows:

1. Develop a model for the decision: Break down the decision into a hierarchy of goals, criteria, and alternatives.

Electronic Supplementary Material The online version of this chapter (https://doi.org/10.1007/978-3-319-68369-0_3) contains supplementary material, which is available to authorized users.

E. Mu, M. Pereyra-Rojas, *Practical Decision Making using Super Decisions v3*, SpringerBriefs in Operations Research, https://doi.org/10.1007/978-3-319-68369-0_3

2. Derive priorities for the criteria: The importance of criteria is compared pairwise with respect to the desired goal to derive their weights. We then check the consistency of judgments; that is, a review of the judgments is done in order to ensure a reasonable level of consistency in terms of proportionality and transitivity.
3. Derive priorities for the alternatives: Derive priorities (preferences) for the alternatives with respect to each criterion (following a similar process as in the previous step, i.e., compare the alternatives pairwise with respect to each criterion). Check and adjust the consistency as required.
4. Synthesize the model: All alternative priorities obtained are combined as a weighted sum—to take into account the weight of each criterion—to establish the overall priorities of the alternatives. The alternative with the highest overall priority constitutes the best choice.
5. Perform sensitivity analysis: A study of how changes in the weights of the criteria could affect the result is done to understand the rationale behind the obtained results.
6. Making a final decision: Based on the synthesis results and sensitivity analysis, a decision can be made.

Next, let us look at each of the above steps using Super Decisions v3.

3.1 Developing a Model

The first step in AHP analysis is to build a hierarchical model for the decision.

When the program starts, a screen showing an information panel on the left and a blank screen panel on the right, the model section, is opened. Here is where you build a hierarchy of the decision. The steps to build the model are:

Press the [+] button at the top left corner of the screen (right above the label "information panel"). A message "Creating new cluster" will appear halfway in the information panel section. Each level of the hierarchy is considered a cluster in Super Decisions lexicon. However, Super Decisions v3 distributes the cluster from left to right (tree view) rather than top down as done in previous software versions. Name the first cluster "Goal" and click "Add more." Repeat this process for each of the clusters. We need to build three groupings or clusters for the Goal, Criteria, and Alternatives[1] corresponding to our example. After creating the last cluster ("Alternatives") you will click "Save" to finish the cluster creation process. You can select any of the clusters and move it around on the blank screen for organization purposes. Figure 3.1 shows the three clusters in our example.

The next step is to create the corresponding elements of the hierarchy (called "nodes" in Super Decisions) within each of the clusters. To create a node in the

[1] Make sure not to misspell the word "Alternatives" otherwise Super Decisions v2 will report an error indicating that the Alternatives are missing in the hierarchical model.

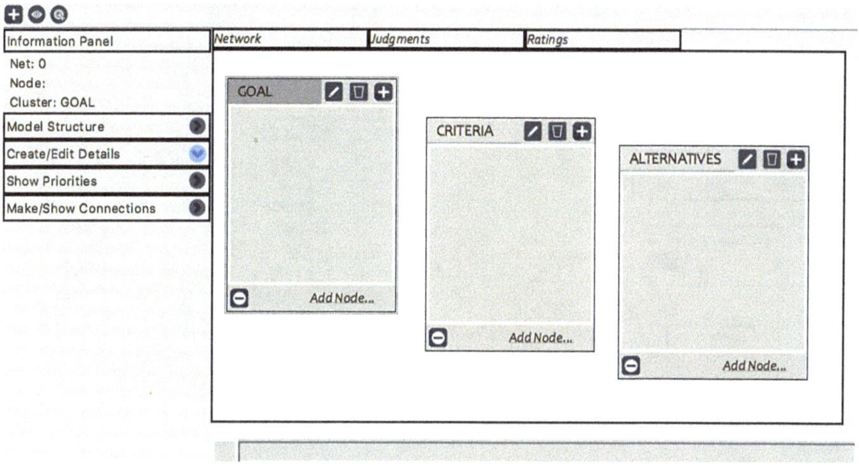

Fig. 3.1 *Clusters* or hierarchy levels for the car purchase example

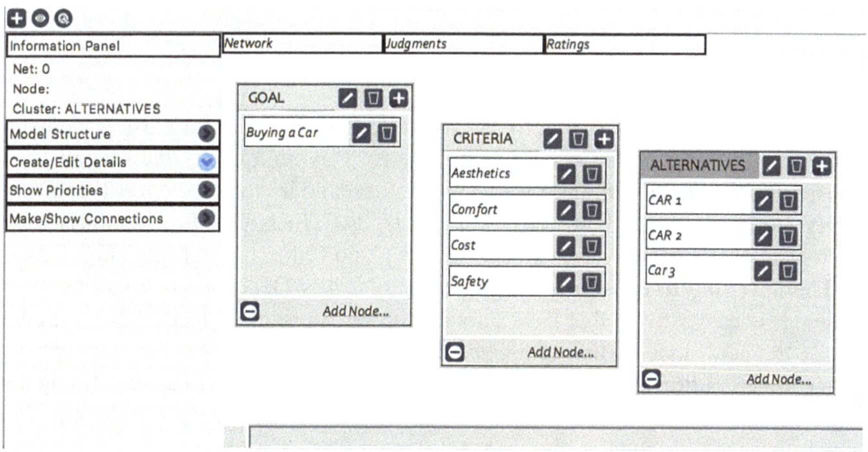

Fig. 3.2 Model clusters with nodes for the car purchase decision

"GOAL" cluster, select this cluster and click the "Add Node…" option in the lower right part of the cluster. This will cause a message "Please set the values for the new node in cluster GOAL" to appear halfway in the information panel (left part of the screen) section. Using the dialog boxes below the display message, name the node as "Buying a Car" and provide any pertinent description. When adding nodes to a cluster, use the "Add more" option until the last node has been added and then use the "Save" option. We have created a node called "Buying a Car" within the cluster Goal. Next, we will repeat this process to create the nodes "cost," "comfort," "safety," and "aesthetic" within the cluster Criteria. Finally, we will create the corresponding nodes "Car 1," "Car 2," and "Car 3" within the cluster Alternatives as shown in Fig. 3.2.

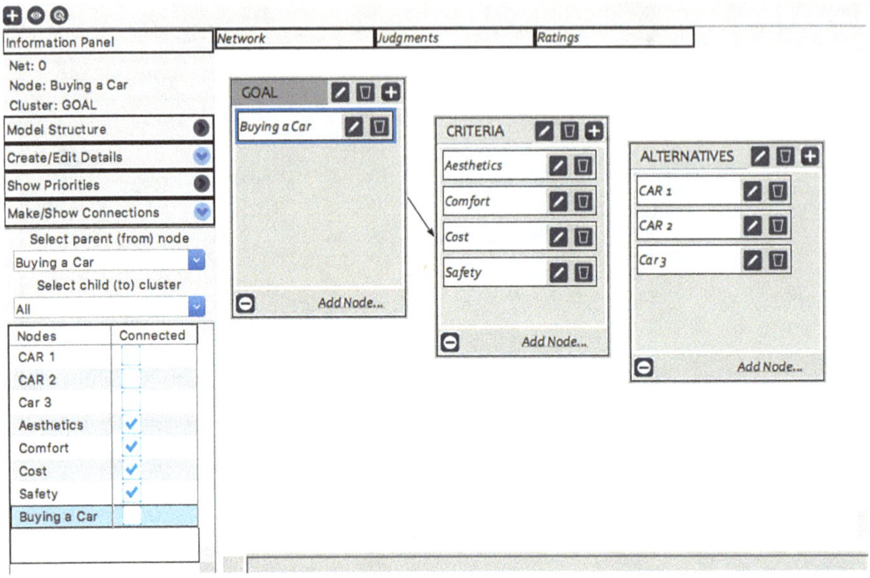

Fig. 3.3 Node connections for "Buying a Car"

The first level of the hierarchy is constituted by the leftmost cluster "GOAL" which has the goal node (in our example, it is "Buying a Car"), the second level (cluster "CRITERIA") contains the specific criteria nodes to be used: cost, comfort, safety, and aesthetics and the third level (cluster "ALTERNATIVES") comprises the alternative nodes to be evaluated: Car 1, Car 2, and Car 3, respectively (Fig. 3.2).

The next step to construct the model using Super Decisions is to connect the nodes. It is easier to do this if we move from left to right. Select (click) with the cursor the goal node ("Buying a Car") in the model, next select the "make/show connections" button in the information panel and a dialog box will appear. Using the cursor select each and all criteria nodes (cost, comfort, aesthetics, and safety) to which you want to connect the node "Buying a Car" as shown in Fig. 3.3.[2] After checking the box of the last node to be connected, click outside the selection area (i.e., in the blank area right below the "buying a car" checkbox option) to ensure it has been properly selected. If this is done, all the checkmarks will look identical as shown in Fig. 3.3.

Once you complete all the desired connections, you can close this dialog by clicking again in the "make/show connections" option. When performing the connections, it is important to keep in mind the following observations:

[2] Be careful not to connect the "Buying a Car" node to any other node but only those corresponding to the criteria. The software allows you to connect any node with any node but AHP modeling requires that the goal node is connected only to the criteria nodes (and each criterion only to the alternatives).

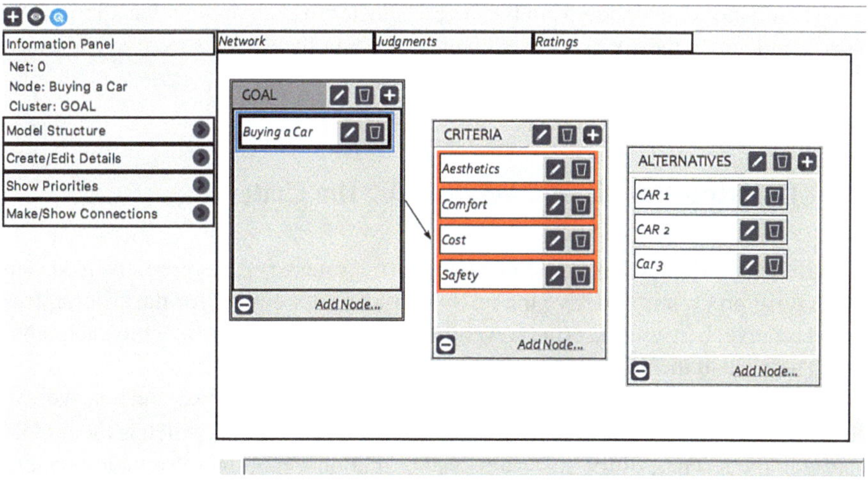

Fig. 3.4 The node "Buying a Car" connected to each criterion

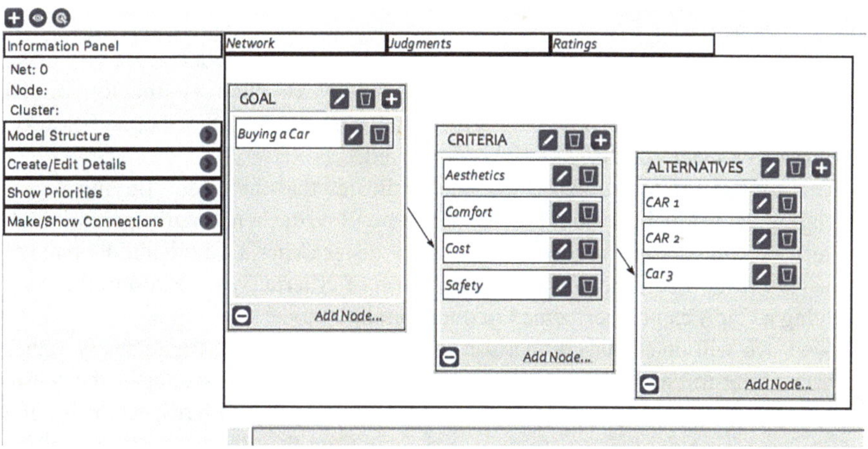

Fig. 3.5 Final hierarchy for "Buying a Car"

Note that to see the connections made, it is required to press the [ ] button, third button from left to right, on the top horizontal bar above "information panel." When pressed, this button will change color to blue [ ]. Then select with the cursor the node "Buying a Car" and the program will frame in red all the nodes "Buying a Car" is connected to. As can be seen in Fig. 3.4, "Buying a Car" is connected to each of the Criteria and nothing else, which is correct for our AHP model. For simplicity, and to avoid congesting the screen, the software only shows a single arrow from the goal cluster to the criteria cluster, instead of three arrows for each connection; however, the red frame clearly identifies the connected nodes.

Next, connect each node from the criteria cluster to each node in the alternatives cluster and verify they are properly connected using the same procedure explained above. The final hierarchy is shown in Fig. 3.5.

3.2 Deriving Priorities (Weights) for the Criteria

Not all the criteria will have the same weight (importance). Therefore, the next step in the AHP process is to derive the relative priorities (weights) for the criteria. It is called relative, because the criteria weights are measured with respect to each other as we will see in the following discussion.

Since we are going to be working on the model we have just created, we can close the information panel section by pressing the [] button (which is the middle button in the left part of the software screen, right on top of the information panel). Consistent with the other icons in this section, it will turn blue when pressed and will cause the information panel section to close to allow more room in the screen for the model itself. We can open/close the information panel section by pressing this icon as needed.

Select with the cursor the "Buying a Car" node in your model so we can make the pairwise comparison of the criteria nodes. Next, click on the top option "Judgments." The screen shown in Fig. 3.6a will appear. We will elaborate below on the three panes (left, center, and right) displayed.

The left side of the screen (Fig. 3.6a) indicates that the node "Buying a car" belonging to the Goal Cluster of the Goal node will be the benchmark against which to pairwise compare the nodes located in the Cluster Criteria. In the middle pane of the screen (Fig. 3.6a), the pairwise comparison of criteria (with regard to the node "Buying a Car") can be performed in questionnaire mode.

Next, we will enter our comparison judgments by selecting the intensity values corresponding to each comparison as shown in Fig. 3.6b. For example, the fourth comparison (indicated by the number 4 on the left) shows that with respect to "Buying a Car," cost is *moderately to strongly more important* than the criterion "Comfort" since an intensity of 4 has been selected on the "Cost" side of the questionnaire. Moreover, "Comfort" is considered very strongly more important than the "Aesthetics" (first comparison in the questionnaire) as it is indicated by the intensity value 7 selected on the "Comfort" side (left part) of the questionnaire in the second comparison. The decision-maker will have to enter the intensity judgments corresponding to each of the six pairwise comparisons until all comparisons have been completed.

A graphical way to see our comparisons is also available by clicking on the tab "Graphical" of the central pane. Figure 3.7 shows the case of the graphical comparison of "Aesthetics" and "Cost." This pane provides the instructions about how to use the graphical interface interactively. Super Decisions v2 allows us to make comparisons in four different ways: graphical, verbal, matrix, and questionnaire, so we may

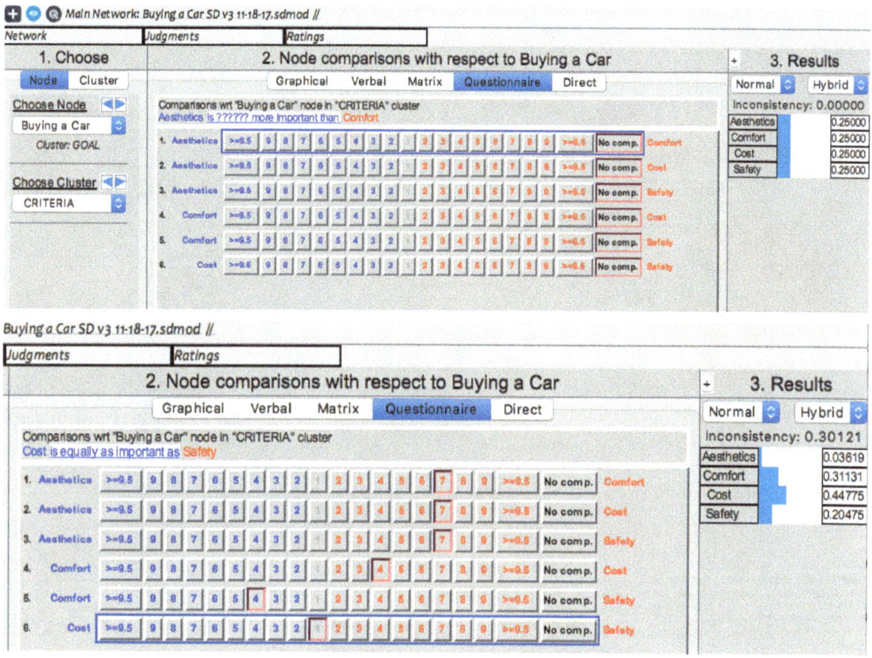

Fig. 3.6 (**a**) Questionnaire mode for comparison of criteria with respect to the "Buying a Car" node. (**b**) Comparison of criteria with respect to the "Buying a Car" node

use the mode that is most natural to us. The verbal comparison of "cost" and "comfort" is shown in Fig. 3.8. You may enter this mode by clicking the corresponding tab "verbal" at the top of the center pane. Note in this Fig. 3.8 that, with respect to our goal of Buying a Car, we have established that the "cost" of the car is from *moderately* to *strongly* more important than "comfort" because the colored selection is between these two judgments. Also notice that we do not need to think of any equivalence of verbal judgments to numerical values because this is done internally by the software.

Each judgment is entered, using the comparison mode of your choice, as shown in the comparison screen (middle pane of Fig. 3.6b). When all comparisons have been made, the calculated priorities appear in the right pane of the comparison interface as shown in Figs. 3.7, 3.8, and 3.9. Accordingly, the cost is the most important criterion with a priority 0.447. However, before accepting these priorities as valid, we must ensure that the consistency ratio is less than 0.10. The right pane of the nodes comparison interface indicates an inconsistency of 0.30, which is much higher than the recommended value of 0.10. This means that we must correct this inconsistency to obtain reliable priorities. The procedure to correct this inconsistency is explained next.

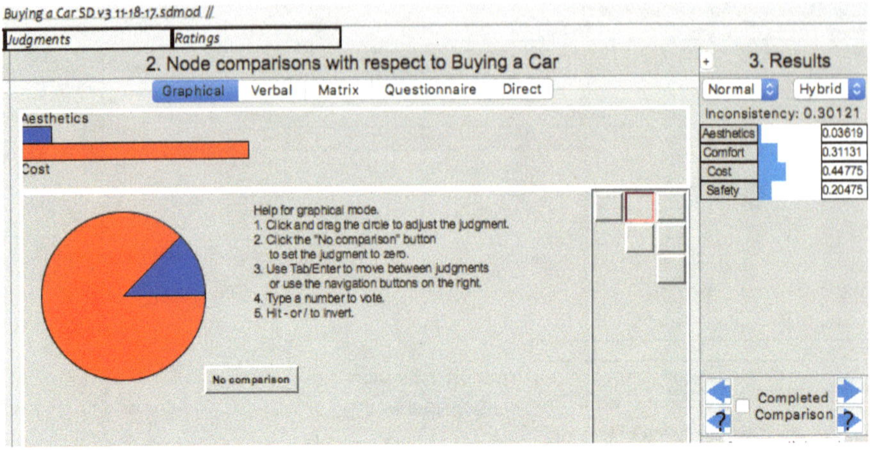

Fig. 3.7 Graphic comparison of two criteria: aesthetics and cost

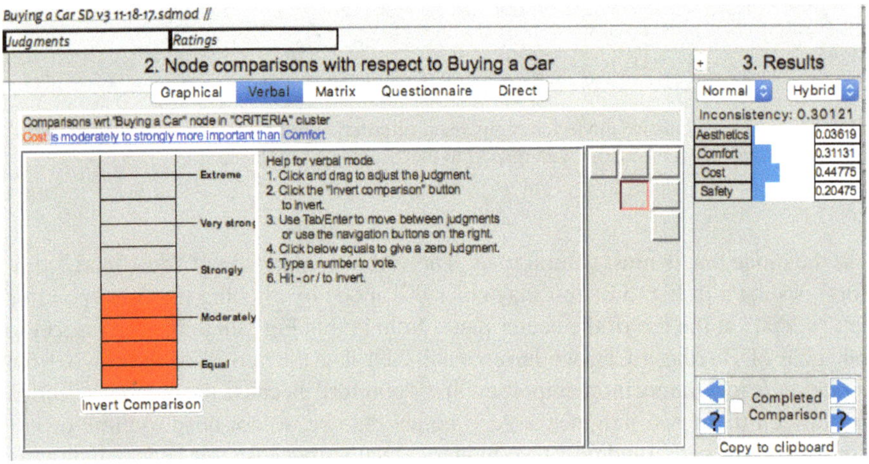

Fig. 3.8 Verbal comparison of two criteria: cost and comfort

3.2.1 Consistency

Super Decisions is particularly useful in adjusting consistency. The calculation of the consistency ratio (CR) is done automatically by the software and displayed as *inconsistency* (0.30121) in the right pane of Figs. 3.6b, 3.7, and 3.8.[3] Since the CR value 0.30 is greater than the commonly accepted maximum value 0.10, we need to adjust our judgments in order to be more consistent and obtain a lower CR.

[3] Super Decisions v2 uses the label inconsistency to refer to AHP consistency ratio.

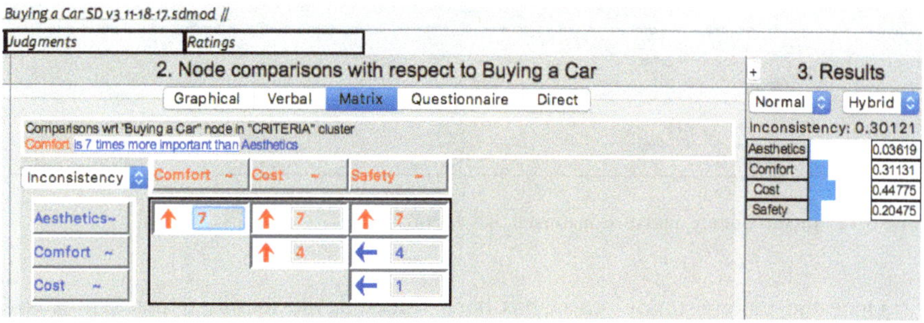

Fig. 3.9 Matrix mode to access inconsistency reports

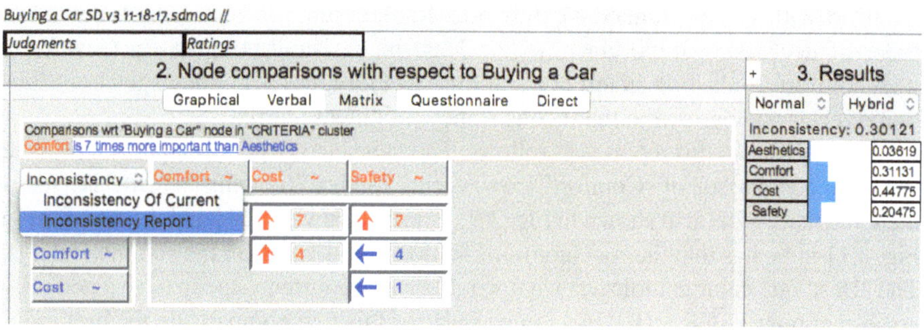

Fig. 3.10 Selecting the inconsistency report

We need to enter the matrix comparison mode by selecting the tab "matrix" at the top of the central pane as shown in Fig. 3.9. This comparison mode can also be used to enter numeric intensities. For this purpose you click on the arrow until it points leftward (if the row criterion is more important than the column criterion) or upwards (if the column criterion is more important than the row criterion). The arrow should point to the most important node and the numeric values indicate the corresponding intensity of preference or importance. The font for the intensity value will be blue when the row is more important than the column (leftward arrow) and red when the column is more important than the row (upward arrow). For the analysis of inconsistency, this matrix mode is important because in this screen, the button "Inconsistency" must be pressed to obtain the inconsistency reports.

Once the inconsistency button is pressed down, a drop-down menu with two options is obtained: *Inconsistency of current* and *Inconsistency Report*, as shown in Fig. 3.10. The first option refers to the level of inconsistency contributed by the judgment currently selected (i.e., the cell where the cursor is currently positioned). The second option provides the overall inconsistency report for the comparison matrix at hand. This inconsistency report provides the contribution of each and all judgments being considered in the matrix to the overall inconsistency. Select the inconsistency report option as shown in Fig. 3.10.

Inconsistency Report

Rank	Row	Col	Current Val	Best Val	Old Inconsist.	New Inconsist.	mprovem
1.	Comfort	Safety	4.000000	1.796568	0.301214	0.070047	76.75 %
2.	Comfort	Cost	4.000000	2.226467	0.301214	0.070047	76.75 %
3.	Cost	Safety	1.000000	4.000000	0.301214	0.187266	37.83 %
4.	Aesthetics	Safety	7.000000	4.873666	0.301214	0.283501	5.88 %
5.	Aesthetics	Cost	7.000000	19.494664	0.301214	0.283501	5.88 %
6.	Aesthetics	Comfort	7.000000	9.803567	0.301214	0.307101	-1.95 %

Fig. 3.11 Inconsistency analysis: inconsistency report

Once the inconsistency report has been selected, the inconsistency report will appear as shown in Fig. 3.11.

The inconsistency report lists all the comparisons in terms of their degree of effect on the overall inconsistency. Starting with the most inconsistent comparison (comfort with safety), ranked #1 (left side, Rank column in Fig. 3.11) followed in order of decreasing importance, to the least inconsistent comparison (aesthetics with comfort, ranked #6 in left column Fig. 3.11). Figure 3.11 shows the contribution of each comparison to the inconsistency judgment matrix.

The way to read this report is as follows: The most inconsistent comparison (ranked #1) is the comparison of "Comfort" (row) versus "Safety" (column) which has a judgment intensity of 4 (also shown in Fig. 3.9). The current value is 4 and the blue font in Fig. 3.11 indicates that the row (comfort) is more important than the column (safety). The "Best Val" column indicates what would be the required value to have a perfectly consistent matrix (CR = 0.0). As can be seen for this first comparison, the best judgment would be to enter a 1.796568 intensity. However, the red font for this value indicates that we would need to invert our preference, that is, making the safety (column) more important than the cost (row) as indicated by the red font for this best value. The report also indicates that if we make this change in the comparison judgments, the current inconsistency (column "Old Inconsist" in Fig. 3.11) of 0.301214 will become 0.070047 ("Best Val" column), corresponding to an improvement of 76.75% in the current inconsistency (column "% improvement" in Fig. 3.11). The report of inconsistency contributions for each of the other five comparisons ("Rank" with values 2–6) is interpreted similarly. Note that an adjustment to any of the first three judgments would have a much greater effect on improving the consistency ratio (76.75% for the first two and 37.83% for the third comparison) than an adjustment to any of the other judgments (see the rightmost column in Fig. 3.11 for expected "% improvement").

Mathematically, the ideal inconsistency adjustment would mean, for example, to assign 1.796 to the comparison comfort-safety (first comparison in the report), making safety more important than comfort. This way, the value of current inconsistency (old inconsistency) 0.301214 would become 0.070047 (new inconsistency). That is, an improvement of 76.75% in the inconsistency. However, to change the recommended value would be opposite of our preference that row comfort is more important than column safety. However, our aim is not to be mathematically perfect but to be honest with

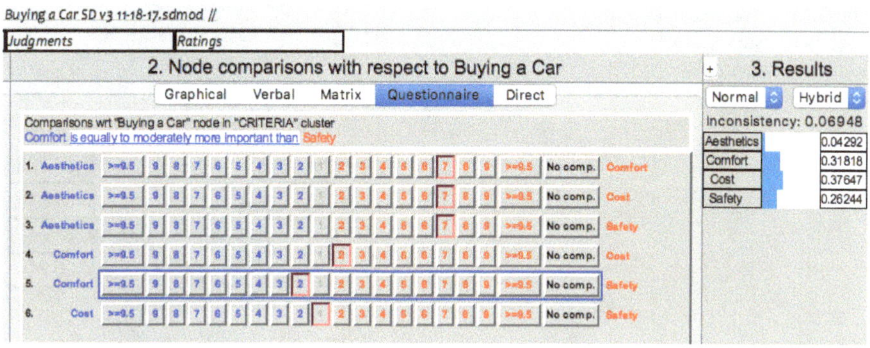

Fig. 3.12 Pairwise comparison matrix adjusted due to inconsistency

our comparisons, maintaining a level of less than 0.10 inconsistency. Hence, we will maintain our judgments that comfort is more important than cost and comfort is more important than safety but to reduce the inconsistency, we will reduce the intensity of our preference from 4 to 2. We will do the same for the case of the comparison comfort-cost (ranked #2 in terms of inconsistency); that is, we will keep our preference that cost is more important but we will also lower the original value from 4 to 2 in the first and second comparisons. Figure 3.12 shows the comparison judgments after these two changes have been made in the questionnaire mode (the reader may want to compare the new judgment intensities corresponding to comfort-cost and comfort-safety with respect to the original values in Fig. 3.6b). Notice that we are just adjusting the intensity of our comparison judgments rather than changing our direction in the preference of which criterion is more important than the other. Still, when looking at Fig. 3.6b (original judgments) and Fig. 3.12 (adjusted judgments) you will notice (in the right pane) that the inconsistency level has changed from 0.30121 (Fig. 3.6b) to 0.06948 (Fig. 3.12), being this last value (0.069) much lower than the 0.10 threshold required for reliable AHP calculations. Super Decisions recalculates the priorities and respective inconsistency, with the result shown, in a closer view for your convenience, in Fig. 3.13.

By making these changes in the comparison matrix, a new value of inconsistency is generated as shown in Fig. 3.13 (right pane of the comparison interface). Note in this figure that the new inconsistency value estimated by the software is 0.06948 which is now less than 0.10; therefore, we can conclude that our judgments matrix has become reasonably consistent for AHP analysis. Also, note that we have maintained our preferences (where comfort is more important than cost and comfort is more important than safety). We have only adjusted the strength of our preferences as can be seen by comparing the new priorities (Fig. 3.13) with the old ones (Fig. 3.6b). In both cases our priorities and magnitudes are similar, except that now the matrix of judgments is more consistent.

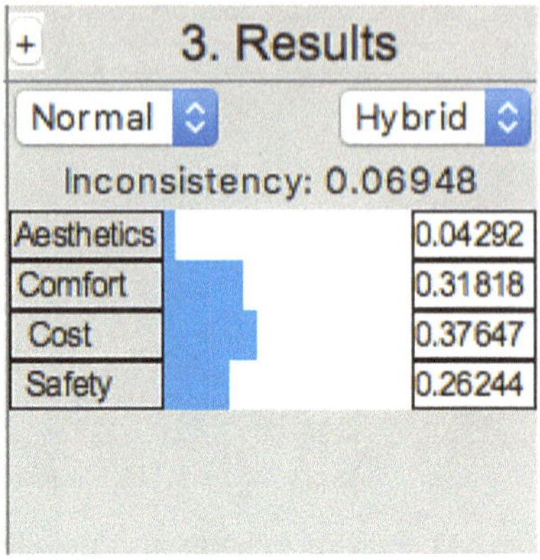

Fig. 3.13 Priorities and final inconsistency after adjusting the pairwise comparison matrix

3.3 Deriving Local Priorities (Preferences) for the Alternatives

Our next step will consist of deriving the relative priorities (preferences) of the alternatives with respect to each criterion. In other words, what are the priorities of the alternatives with respect to aesthetics, cost, comfort, and safety, respectively? Since these priorities are valid only with respect to each specific criterion, they are called local priorities to differentiate them from the overall or general priorities to be calculated later.

We will need to get back to our network (model) view and for this purpose we will select the option "Network" which is the first left tab. The "Network" tab allows us to get back and forth to our network (model) view.

The next step is to prioritize the alternatives according to each of the criteria (one at the time). For example, based solely on the criterion *cost*, it is required to determine which is the preference (or local priority) of each alternative. Next, the pairwise comparison process is done taking into account only the criterion comfort and so on until the alternatives have been prioritized against all the criteria.

Select the criteria node *Cost* (by clicking the cursor on Cost) as shown in Fig. 3.14. Notice that the selected parent node for the comparison (criterion "Cost") is highlighted by a blue frame. Next click the tab "Judgments" (second tab on the top menu bar, circled in an oval in Fig. 3.14), as we did earlier, to get into the comparison mode. You may select any of the comparison modes shown in the horizontal bar (graphical, verbal, matrix, questionnaire, and direct). For our example, we will enter our judgments in questionnaire mode and we will obtain the screen shown in Fig. 3.15 (only the left and center panel are shown for convenience).

We now proceed to compare alternatives in pairs using the questionnaire mode (unless you prefer the graphical, verbal, or matrix comparison mode) as shown in Fig. 3.15 (middle pane of the comparison interface). This figure shows the specific case of pairwise comparison of different alternatives with respect to cost. Figure 3.16 (right pane of the comparison interface) shows the local priorities of the alternatives with respect to this single criterion of cost. This process is repeated for each of the other criteria in the model.

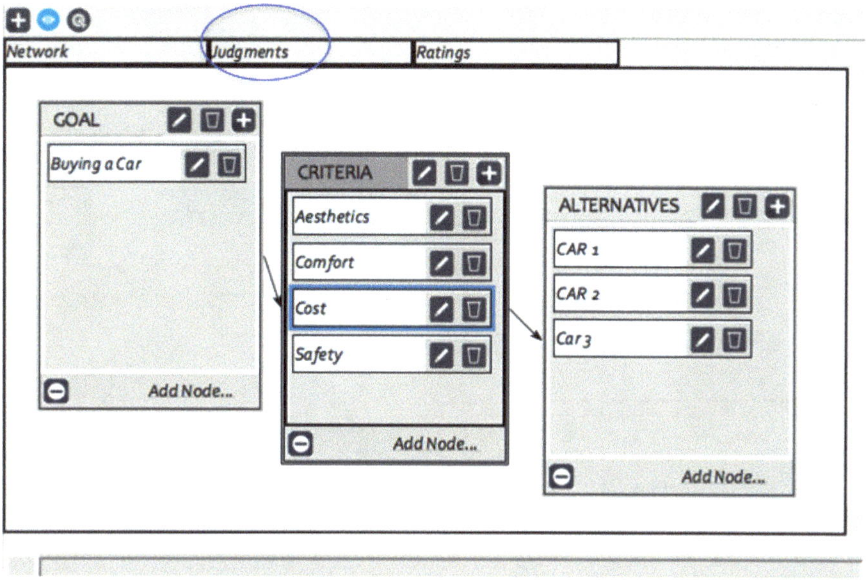

Fig. 3.14 Selecting the comparison of alternatives with respect to cost

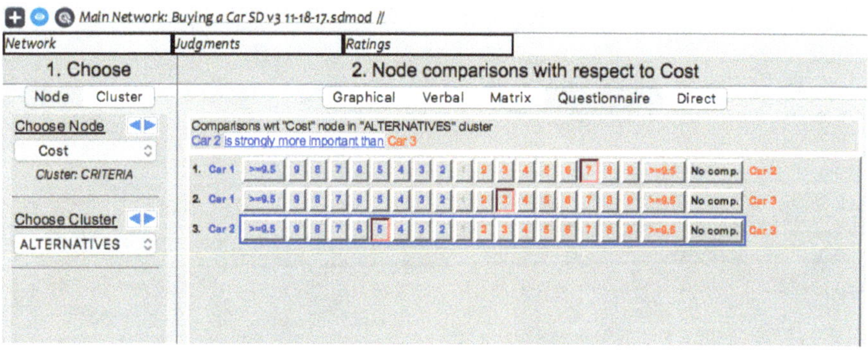

Fig. 3.15 Comparing alternatives with respect to the criterion cost

Figures 3.17, 3.18, and 3.19 show comparisons (middle pane "2. Node comparisons with respect to…") and local priorities of the alternatives (right pane "3. Results") with respect to each one of the criteria in the model.[4] After you have completed all the comparisons, you may want to get back to your model view by clicking again on "Network."

[4] One healthy practice is that upon completing the judgments in a given comparison matrix, you check the box "Completed comparison" on the lower right part of the screen. At the end, when you have entered judgments in all your comparison matrices following this procedure, you can go to the top bar menu, select "Computations" followed by "Sanity Check" and the software will indicate you if there is any comparison matrix you did not work upon (i.e., where the "Completed Comparison" box is unchecked).

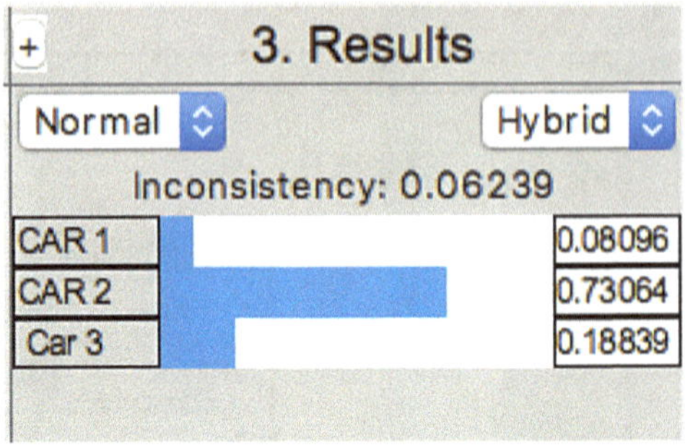

Fig. 3.16 Priorities of the alternatives with respect to the criterion cost

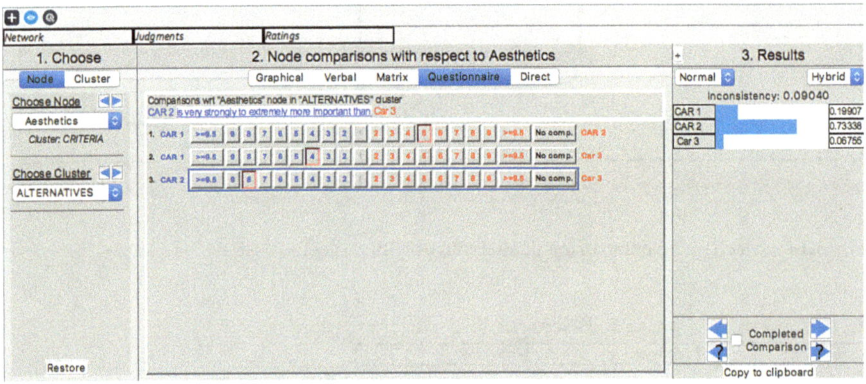

Fig. 3.17 Comparison of alternatives with respect to aesthetics

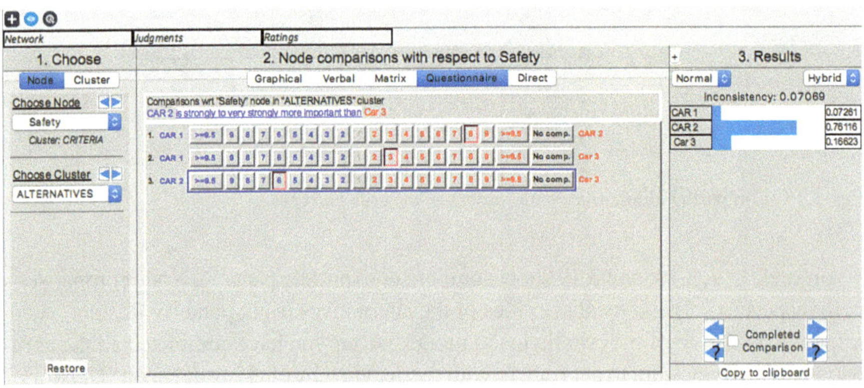

Fig. 3.18 Comparison of the alternatives with respect to safety

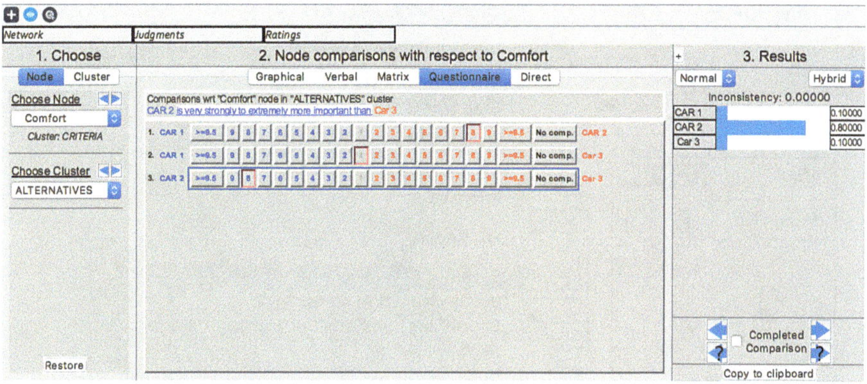

Fig. 3.19 Comparison of the alternatives with respect to comfort

3.4 Deriving Overall Priorities (Model Synthesis)

Now we need to work on the overall synthesis process; that is, we need to determine the general priorities of alternatives taking into account the level of importance we have assigned to the criteria.

The synthesis is performed from the main window of the entire model. Select the option *Computations* (from the bar menu at the very top in your computer screen) and then *synthesize* as shown in Fig. 3.20. Figure 3.21 shows the result of this process. In Fig. 3.21 we can see, under the *Normals* column, that the alternative with highest priority, for this example, is the Car 2 (0.760837); followed by the Car 3 (0.149266) and the Car 1 (0.089896).

The *Normals* column in Fig. 3.21 shows the general or overall priorities, also called final preferences, in standardized form. According to this column, Car 2 has 76% of the preference, based on the comparisons made. The *Ideals* column is obtained by dividing each value in the *Normals* column by the highest value of said column (0.760837 in this example). Thus the highest priority has a value of 1 (=0.760837/0.760837) or 100%. This indicates, for example, that the second best option, Car 3, is 14.9% (=0.14927/0.760837) as good as the best (ideal) option.[5]

We can also display the overall priorities (Fig. 3.21) together with the weights of the criteria on the same synthesis screen as shown in Fig.3.22. To obtain this display, we select again *Computations* but this time followed by *Priorities* (instead of Synthesis) from the drop-down menu in Fig. 3.20.

[5]The *Raw* column in the priorities screenshot (rightmost column not shown in Fig. 3.22) is not used for AHP analysis.

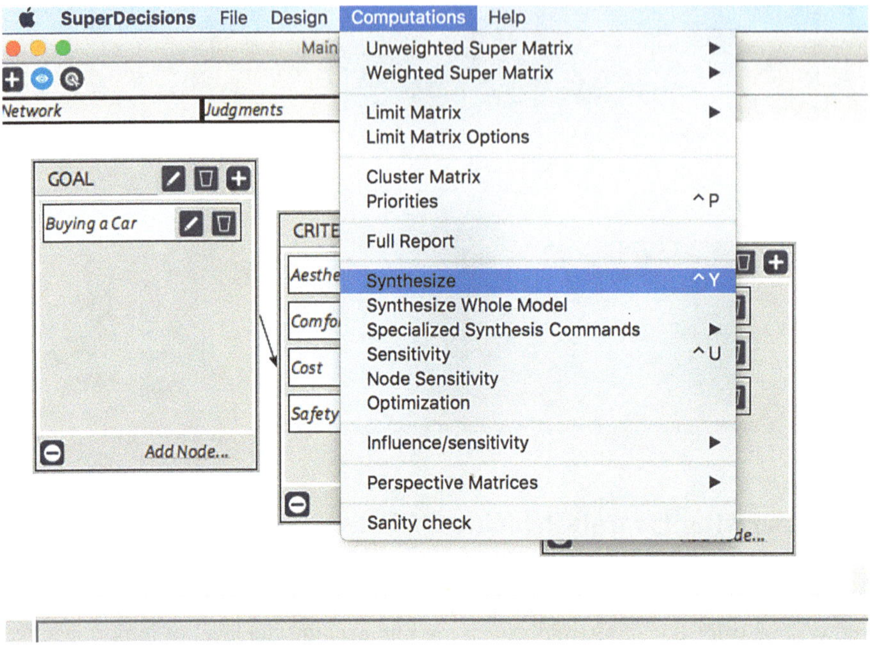

Fig. 3.20 Selecting the option synthesize

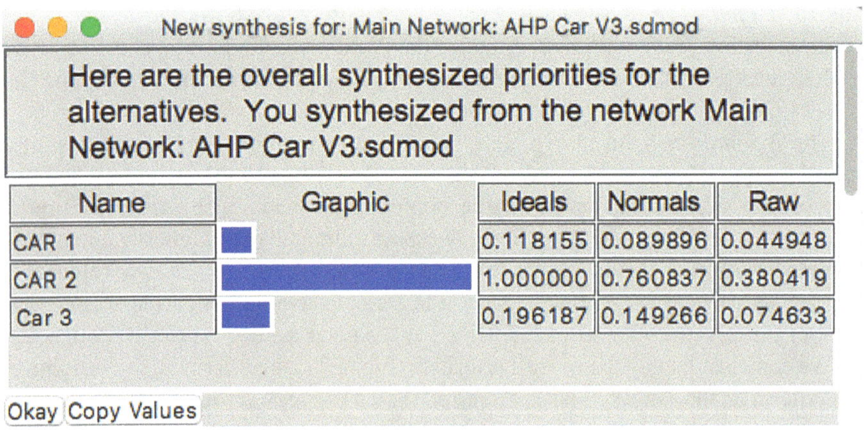

Fig. 3.21 Overall priorities as a result of the synthesis

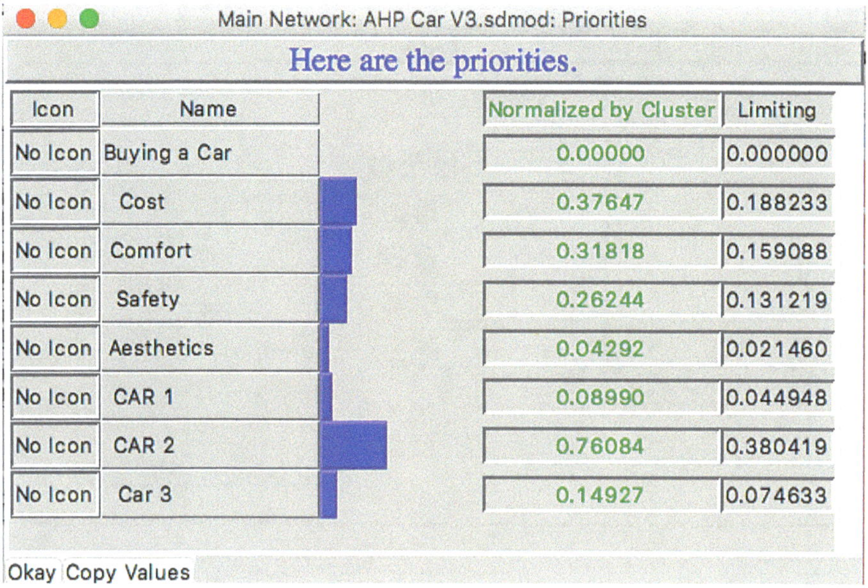

Fig. 3.22 Priorities of the alternatives and criteria

3.5 Sensitivity Analysis

The final priorities of the alternatives will be heavily influenced by the weights given to the respective criteria. It is useful to perform a "what-if" analysis to see how the final results would have changed if the weights of the criteria would have been different.

For this reason, the last step in the evaluation of alternatives is to perform a sensitivity analysis. This analysis is performed to investigate how sensitive the results are with respect to the importance we have derived for the different criteria. Although there are different ways to perform the sensitivity analysis using Super Decisions v3, we will provide a simple and practical way to perform this, given the intended scope of this book.

In the model view (obtained by clicking on "Network"), select (mouse left-click) the goal node "Buying a Car" and then click on the "Judgment" tab in the bar menu—circled with an oval, as shown in Fig. 3.23—to get into the comparison mode of criteria with respect to the goal node. Next, click the tab "direct" to choose the direct comparison mode shown in Fig. 3.24. Notice that the criteria weights in this figure correspond to the derived criteria priorities. In other words, this is our original analysis scenario previously obtained. However, direct mode is not simply a different way to present the criteria priorities. It also allows us to change the priority values directly.

We could be interested in knowing if Car 2 would have been the best choice if all the criteria would have had the same weight. To check this scenario, we first save our original scenario file with a name such as "Buying a Car Original Scenario."

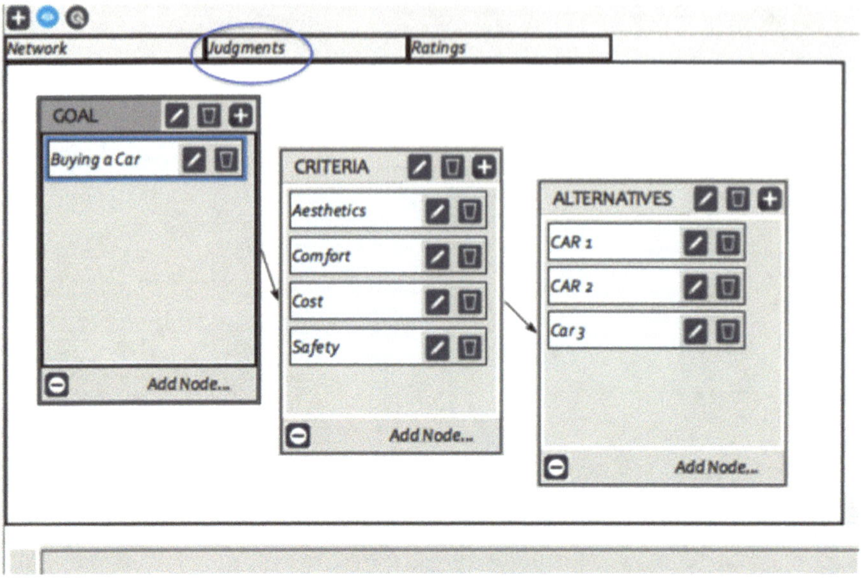

Fig. 3.23 Selecting comparison of criteria ("Judgments") with respect to "Buying a Car"

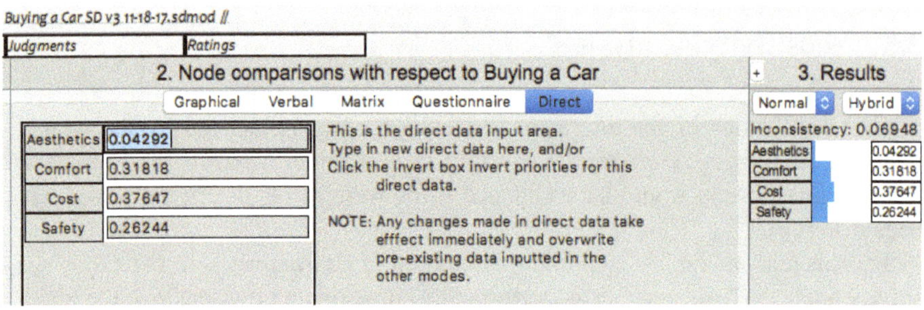

Fig. 3.24 "Buying a Car" original scenario shown in direct mode

Select *File* > *SaveAs* from the bar menu at the very top of your computer screen. Next, we can open it again and save it as "Buying a Car Sensitivity Scenario 1" or similar name. Next, in the direct mode in Fig. 3.24 we will enter the value 0.25 as a weight for each of the criteria.[6] To do this enter 0.25 in the first cell and hit "Enter" or "Return" in your keyboard. The cursor will move to the next cell. Enter 0.25 again and click "Enter." Repeat this process until all cells have the same 0.25 value (make sure this is the case by inspecting the cells visually) and you will obtain the

[6] Given that there are 4 criteria, the way to distribute the weights equally among them is by performing the calculation 1/ 4 = 0.25. Should there be 5 criteria, the weight to distribute equally would be 1/5 = 0.2 and so on.

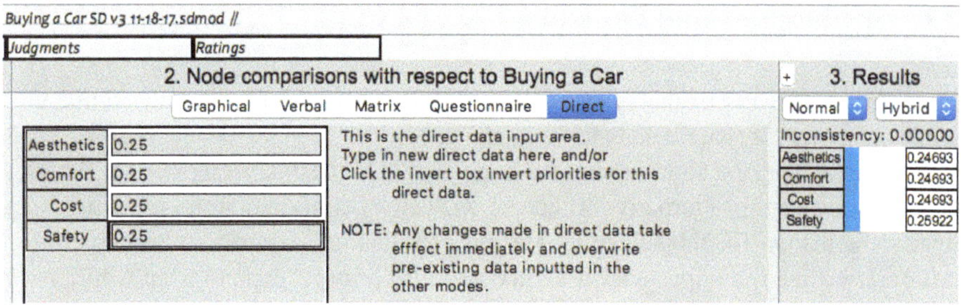

Fig. 3.25 Direct mode with criteria with equal weight

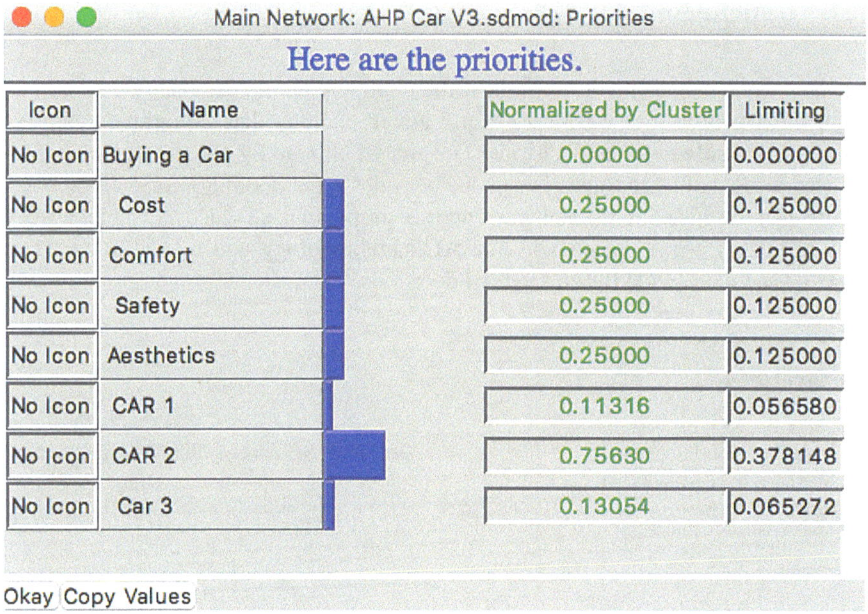

Fig. 3.26 All criteria are equally important

screen shown in Fig. 3.25. Go to the top menu of the software and select *Computations* > *Priorities* (in the drop-down menu from Fig. 3.20) to obtain the screen shown in Fig. 3.26.

As can be seen from Fig. 3.26, if all criteria are equally important our best choice is still the Car 2 while the other two alternatives are still quite behind. We can analyze different possible scenarios of interest to understand in which cases the best original choice is no longer so.

3.6 Making a Final Decision

Based on the results of the synthesis and the insight obtained from the sensitivity analysis, a final decision needs to be made.

In general, the best alternative is the one with the highest general priority. The user can now choose this alternative (if he/she wishes to do so) and at the same time can justify the reason for the selection. He/she now has the opportunity to explain the criteria used and the importance assigned and furthermore, explain what would have happened if the weights of the criteria had changed.

3.7 Conclusion

In short, we have seen that because of the cognitive anomalies that we, as human beings, experience, it is necessary to use a methodology that is intuitively simple, efficient, and safe to make decisions. The analytic hierarchy process (AHP) implemented in the software Super Decisions provides a methodology for making decisions in an intuitive but rational way and it is simple to use (Videos 3.1, 3.2, 3.3, 3.4 and 3.5). This is the reason why the AHP methodology and related software is widely used worldwide for all kinds of decisions.

References

Creative Decisions Foundation. (2017). *Creative Decisions Foundation*. Retrieved from http://www.creativedecisions.net

Super Decisions. (2017). *Super Decisions*. Retrieved from http://sdbeta.superdecisions.com

Suggested Reading[7]

Developing a Model in Super Decisions v3 https://mix.office.com/watch/1mp07zua2di3p

Deriving Priorities for Criteria in Super Decisions v3 https://mix.office.com/watch/1qr5h5rqp9itw

Deriving Local Priorities for Alternatives in SD v3 https://mix.office.com/watch/1sixhmswitqxo

Deriving Overall Priorities in Super Decisions v3 https://mix.office.com/watch/1t5ve54yjkpe5

Performing Sensitivity Analysis in Super Decisions v3 https://mix.office.com/watch/1k6dt0sa7047a

[7]These videos are the same as those provided in the supplementary material section but the links below are provided as alternative links and for redundancy purposes.

Part II
Intermediate

Chapter 4
AHP Models with Sub-criteria Using v3

Abstract In many situations, it is necessary to add sub-criteria to one or more of the original criteria. The process is very straightforward as it will be shown here. Also, readers are encouraged to review all the Super Decisions documentation provided by the software developer (www.superdecisions.com).

4.1 Introducing Sub-criteria in AHP Super Decision Models

Let us assume that for the Buying Car example (shown in Fig. 4.1), we realized upon building the criteriacluster that we need to add sub-criteria to the cost criterion.

For this purpose, we select the icon at the top left corner of the screen (above "Information Panel") to add a new cluster that we will call "Cost Sub-criteria" and then "Save." Next, click "Add node…" in the cost sub-criteria cluster and proceed to add the sub-criterion "Acquisition Cost" using the dialog box in the information panel, click "Add more" and enter the sub-criterion "Maintenance Cost." You will obtain the screen shown in Fig. 4.2.

Our next step is to connect the cost criterion to the corresponding sub-criteria nodes. For this purpose, we select the cost node in the model diagram and click the option "Make/Show Connections" on the information panel on the left. Make sure that the selected "Parent node (From) node" is "Cost" and using the drop-down menu select the "Child (To) Cluster" called "Cost Sub-criteria" as shown in the information panel section in Fig. 4.3. Next, select the checkboxes of the corresponding "Cost" sub-criteria to complete the connection of the criteria node "Cost" to its respective sub-criteria "Acquisition Cost" and "Maintenance Cost" and you will obtain the screen shown in Fig. 4.4.

We can now close the connection dialog but clicking again "Make/Show Connections." To verify our model visually, press the button from the top model menu (after pressed, its color will change to light blue) and select the cost criterion node to see what nodes cost is connected to. As can be seen in Fig. 4.5, the cost criterion node is connected to the sub-criteria nodes acquisition cost and maintenance

Electronic Supplementary Material The online version of this chapter (https://doi.org/10.1007/978-3-319-68369-0_4) contains supplementary material, which is available to authorized users.

E. Mu, M. Pereyra-Rojas, *Practical Decision Making using Super Decisions v3*, SpringerBriefs in Operations Research, https://doi.org/10.1007/978-3-319-68369-0_4

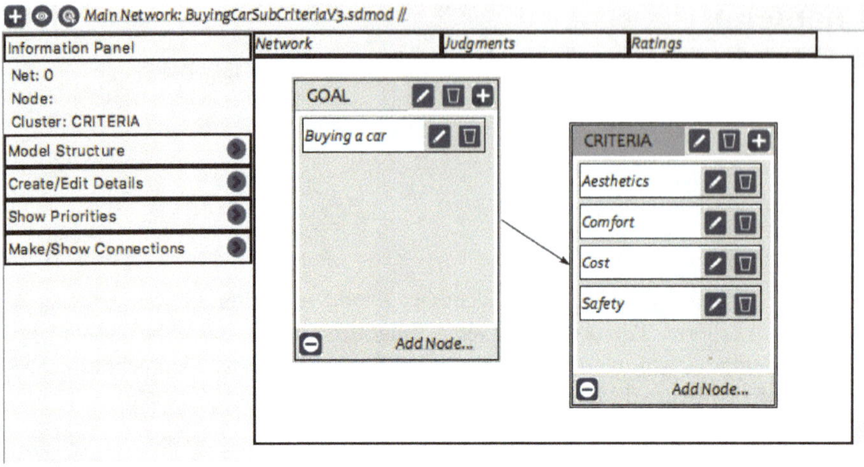

Fig. 4.1 Buying a Car model with criteria only

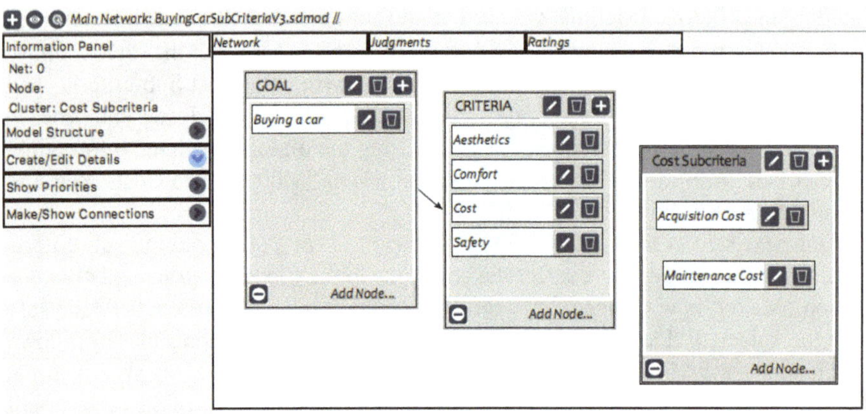

Fig. 4.2 Addition of cost sub-criteria

cost as indicated by the fact that these two nodes are highlighted in red. This confirms that our sub-criteria connections have been properly made.

We can also verify that our goal node is in turn connected to the criteria. Select the goal node "Buying a Car" and see what nodes in the model it is connected to by inspecting which nodes are framed in red. You will notice that, as shown in Fig. 4.6, the node "Buying a Car" is connected to the criteria nodes: cost, comfort, safety, and aesthetics. This is expected because we started this example assuming that this top

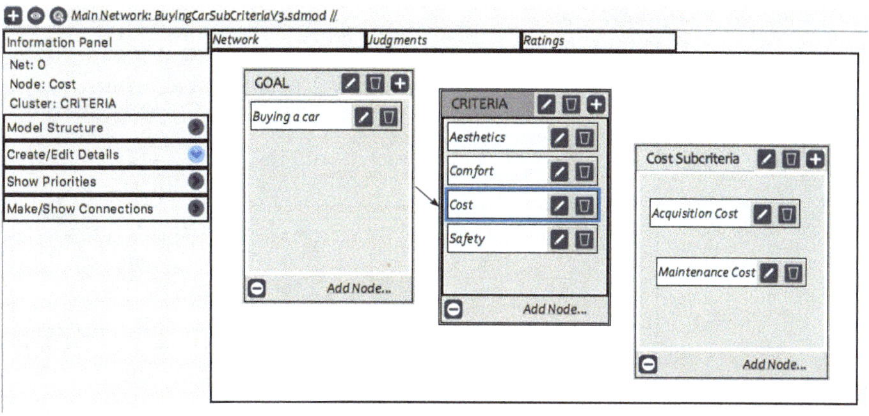

Fig. 4.3 Selecting the "Node Connections" option

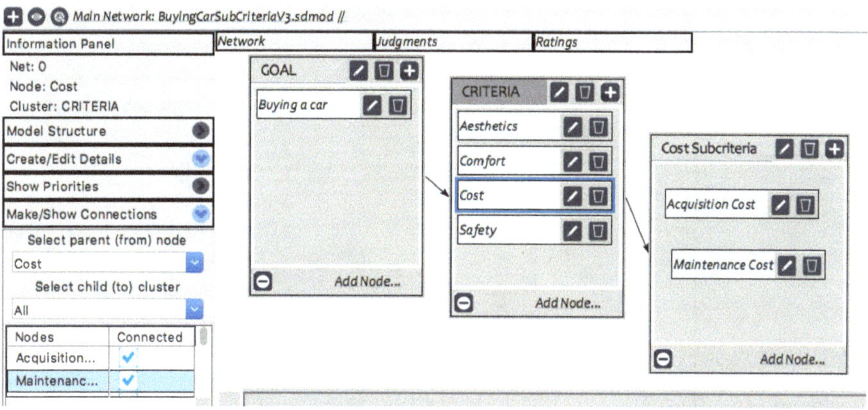

Fig. 4.4 Connecting "Cost" to its sub-criteria

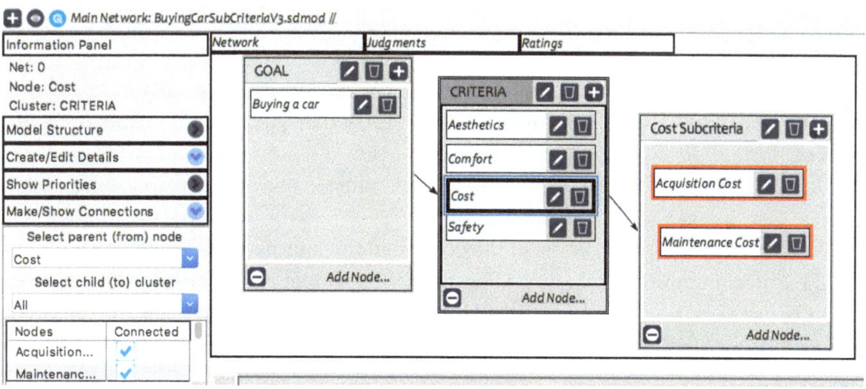

Fig. 4.5 Verifying cost connections to its sub-criteria

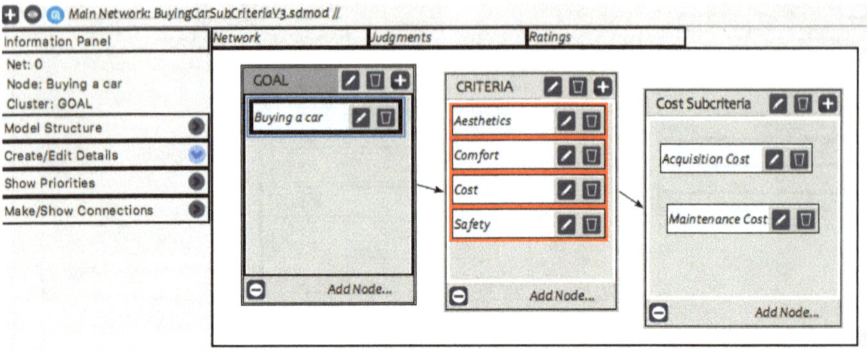

Fig. 4.6 Verifying "Buying a Car" connections to its criteria

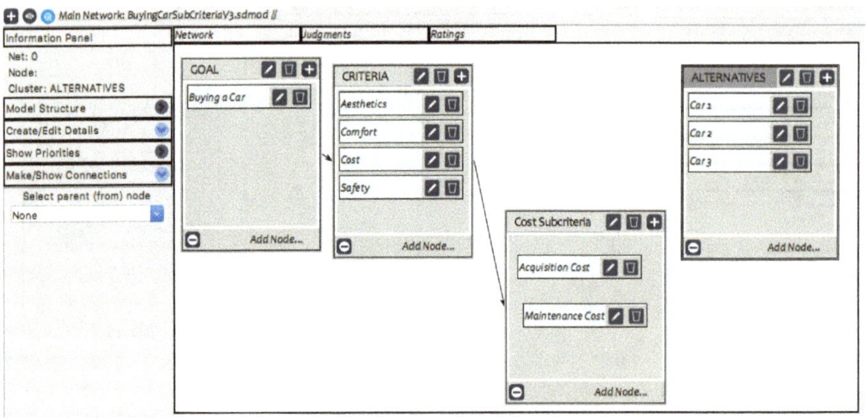

Fig. 4.7 Model screenshot prior to connecting the alternatives

part of the model had been completed and pairwise compared to obtain the criteria weights. Still, it is always very important to verify that your model connections are correct.

Now, we proceed to create the alternatives cluster and its corresponding nodes (Car 1, Car 2, and Car 3) as shown in Fig. 4.7.

We now are required to connect the criteria to the alternatives. We will do so only for the criteria: comfort, safety, and aesthetics as shown in Fig. 4.8. Notice that we do NOT connect the cost node given that it has sub-criteria. In this case, it is the cost sub-criteria that will be connected to the alternatives.

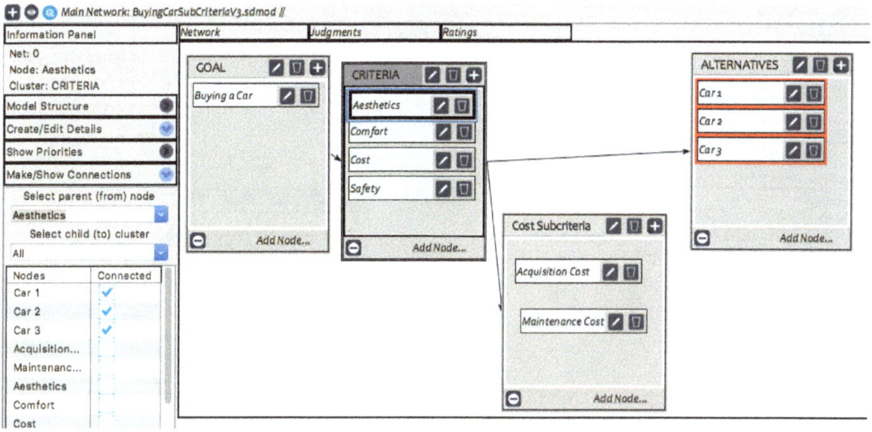

Fig. 4.8 Verifying connections from criteria (except cost) to the alternatives

Select the "acquisition cost" sub-criteria node and press "Make/Show Connections" and select the checkboxes corresponding to the three alternatives Car 1, Car 2, and Car 3, to connect the acquisition cost to all three alternatives. To verify that the connections were properly made, select the [ ] position the cursor on top of the acquisition cost sub-criterion and you will obtain the screen shown in Fig.4.9 which confirms that acquisition cost is connected to all the alternatives, as indicated by the red highlights in Fig. 4.9.

Repeat the same procedure to connect the maintenance cost sub-criterion node to each of the alternatives. Once completed, verify this node is properly connected to the alternatives as shown in Fig. 4.10.

The top criteria cost, comfort, safety, and aesthetics must be compared pairwise to obtain their weights, ensuring that the comparison matrix inconsistencyis less than or equal to 0.1. As can be seen in Fig. 4.11, the criteria pairwise comparisons have been completed and the criteria weights have been obtained (rightmost pane labeled "3. Results") with an inconsistency of 0.06948 which is much less than 0.1.

Now we need to compare pairwise the cost sub-criteria: acquisition cost and maintenance cost with respect to their cost criterion node. For this purpose, click on "Network" in the horizontal menu to get back to our model, next select the "Cost" criterion and "Judgements" and this will get the screenshot shown in Fig. 4.12. In this example, maintenance cost is strongly more important than acquisition cost with respect to the cost. The results (right pane) indicate that maintenance cost has a weight of 0.833 while acquisition cost has 0.166. Also, notice that the inconsistency is 0.000 because we only have two sub-criteria to compare. However, if we had three or more sub-criteria we would most likely have obtained an inconsistency different from 0. In this case, ensuring that this

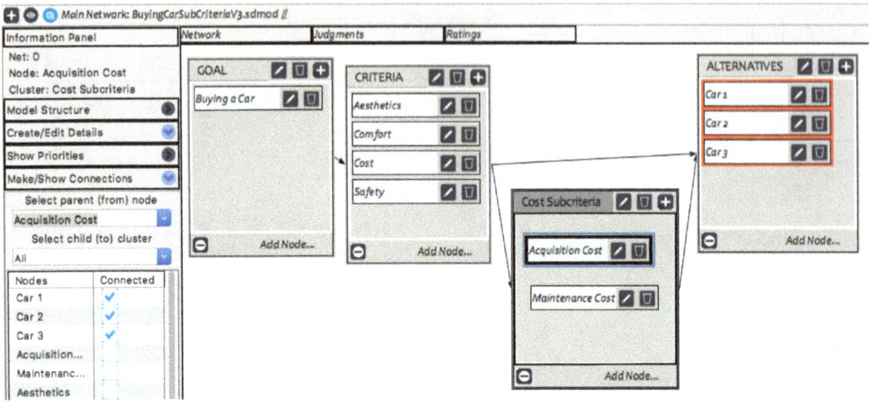

Fig. 4.9 Verifying connection from "Acquisition Cost" to alternatives

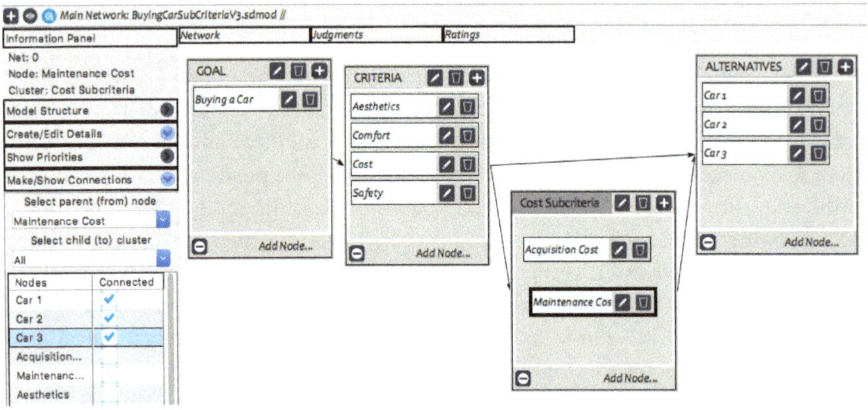

Fig. 4.10 Verifying connection from "Maintenance Cost" to alternatives

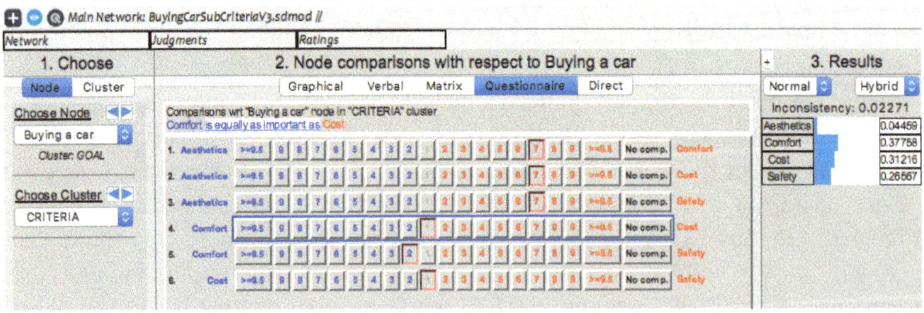

Fig. 4.11 Pairwise comparison of criteria

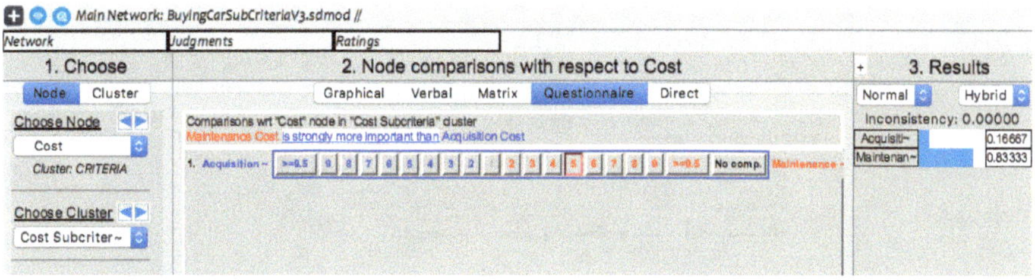

Fig. 4.12 Pairwise comparison of cost sub-criteria with respect to "Cost"

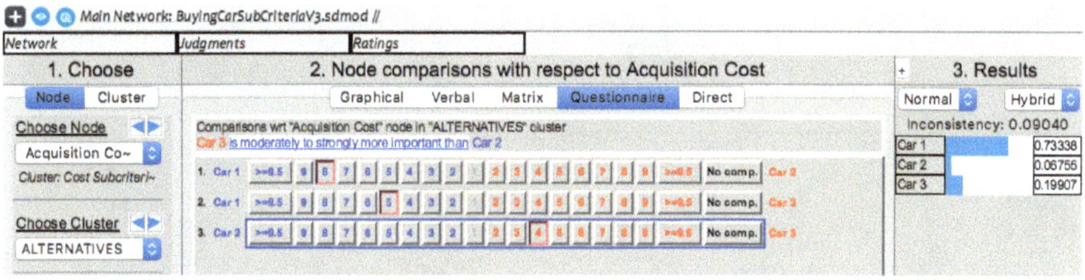

Fig. 4.13 Comparison of alternatives with respect to "Acquisition Cost"

inconsistency was less than or equal to 0.1 is important and any correction to the judgments should be made if needed.

Next, we compare the alternatives pairwise with respect to each criterion. However, in the case of cost, we will compare the alternatives against the cost sub-criteria. For this purpose, we first select "Network" to get to our model, next we select the sub-criterion node acquisition cost, click on "Judgements" and we enter the appropriate comparison judgments to obtain the screen shown in Fig. 4.13. The results (right pane) show that Car 1 has the highest preference (0.733) with respect to acquisition costs. Also, the inconsistency level (0.090) is acceptable (<=0.1); therefore no inconsistency analysis and comparison adjustments are required (Video 4.1)

We repeat the same procedure to compare the alternatives with respect to the sub-criteria node Maintenance Cost as shown in Fig. 4.14. Again, we verify that the inconsistency level is acceptable (0.06239 < = 0.1) before accepting the results indicating that Car 1 is the best choice (0.730) with respect to maintenance costs as shown in Fig. 4.14.

Next, we repeat the pairwise evaluation of the alternatives with respect to the other criteria comfort, safety, and aesthetics, as shown in Figs. 4.15, 4.16, and 4.17.

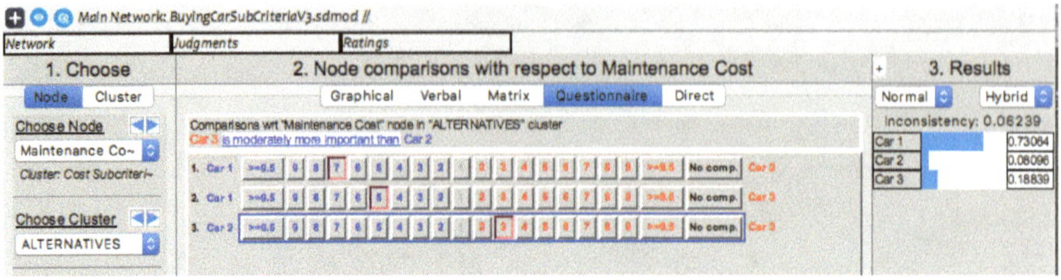

Fig. 4.14 Comparison of alternatives with respect to "Maintenance Cost"

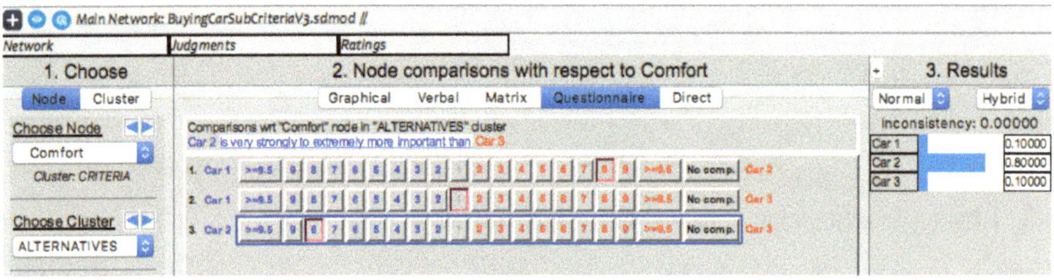

Fig. 4.15 Comparison of alternatives with respect to "Comfort"

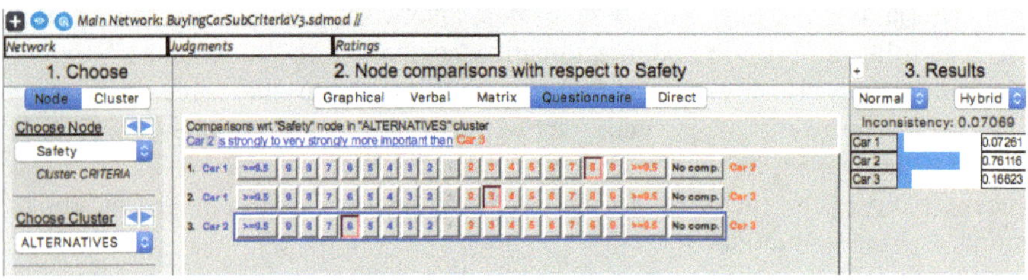

Fig. 4.16 Comparison of alternatives with respect to "Safety"

The final step is to obtain the final priorities by selecting from the top menu, Computations > Priorities to obtain the results shown in Fig. 4.18. This figure shows all the priorities (under the heading "Normalized by Cluster") obtained in the decision model.

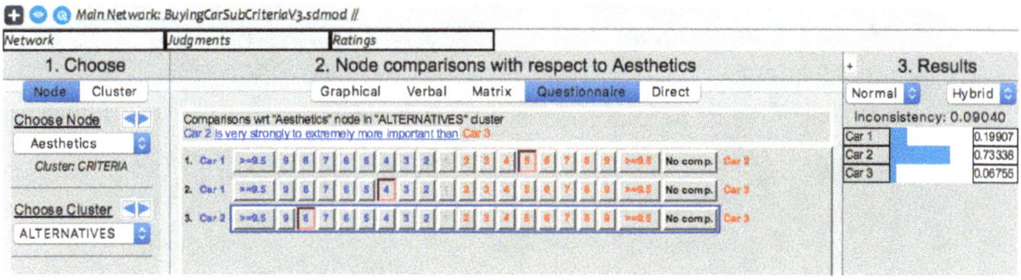

Fig. 4.17 Comparison of alternatives with respect to "Aesthetics"

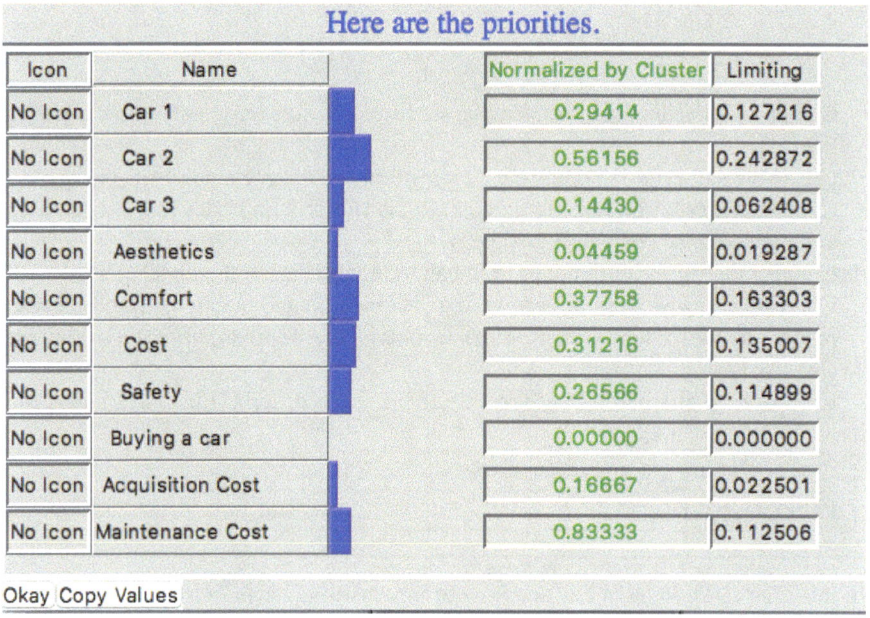

Here are the priorities.

Icon	Name	Normalized by Cluster	Limiting
No Icon	Car 1	0.29414	0.127216
No Icon	Car 2	0.56156	0.242872
No Icon	Car 3	0.14430	0.062408
No Icon	Aesthetics	0.04459	0.019287
No Icon	Comfort	0.37758	0.163303
No Icon	Cost	0.31216	0.135007
No Icon	Safety	0.26566	0.114899
No Icon	Buying a car	0.00000	0.000000
No Icon	Acquisition Cost	0.16667	0.022501
No Icon	Maintenance Cost	0.83333	0.112506

Okay Copy Values

Fig. 4.18 Priorities for criteria, sub-criteria, and alternatives

To focus only on the priorities obtained for the alternatives, select *Computations* > *Synthesize* to obtain the results shown in Fig. 4.19.

In summary, the procedure to insert sub-criteria to a specific criterion (e.g., cost in Fig. 4.1) consists of[1]:

[1] We are summarizing here only the insertion of sub-criteria, not the analysis of the whole model as was done in a previous chapter.

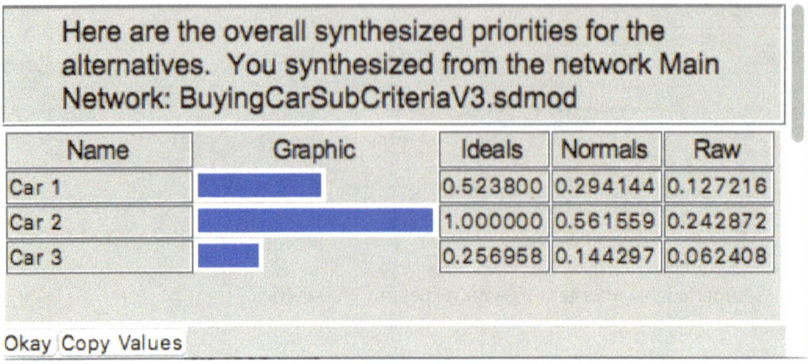
Here are the overall synthesized priorities for the alternatives. You synthesized from the network Main Network: BuyingCarSubCriteriaV3.sdmod

Name	Graphic	Ideals	Normals	Raw
Car 1		0.523800	0.294144	0.127216
Car 2		1.000000	0.561559	0.242872
Car 3		0.256958	0.144297	0.062408

Okay Copy Values

Fig. 4.19 Synthesized priorities for the "Buying a Car" example

- Create a sub-criteria cluster for the specific criterion (e.g., cost sub-criteria in Fig. 4.2)
- Create the sub-criteria nodes (e.g., acquisition and maintenance costs in Fig. 4.2)
- Connect the criterion node (e.g., cost) to the sub-criteria nodes (e.g., acquisition and maintenance costs in Fig. 4.5)
- Connect the sub-criteria nodes to the alternatives (Figs. 4.9 and 4.10)
- Compare pairwise the sub-criteria (e.g., acquisition and maintenance costs) with respect to the criterion (e.g., cost) to obtain the relative sub-criteria weights (Figs. 4.12)
- Compare the alternatives with respect to these sub-criteria (Figs. 4.13 and 4.14)

4.2 Conclusion

In this chapter, you have learned how to insert sub-criteria in a Super Decisions Model (Video 4.1). Notice that the alternatives are compared against the lower nodes of the hierarchy, independently of these nodes being criteria or sub-criteria. In our example, the alternatives were compared against acquisition cost, maintenance cost, comfort, safety, and aesthetics where the first two nodes were sub-criteria. Which nodes the alternatives are compared against is determined by the top-down connections of criteria/sub-criteria to the alternatives (Video 4.2).

Suggested Reading[2]

Introducing Sub-Criteria in Super Decisions v3 https://mix.office.com/watch/1t6nwax0l4w3y

Pairwise Comparisons with Sub-criteria in Super Decisions v3 https://mix.office.com/watch/3nq9bvfgpq4c

[2]These videos are the same as those provided in the supplementary material section but the links below are provided as alternative links and for redundancy purposes.

Chapter 5
Understanding Ratings Models

Abstract Up to now we have discussed AHP *relative models*, that is, models in which both the criteria and alternatives are prioritized through pairwise comparison.

Up to now we have discussed AHP *relative models*, that is, models in which both the criteria and alternatives are prioritized through pairwise comparison. However, sometimes there is a large number of alternatives to consider. For example, in the case of evaluating employees for promotion, it would not be unusual to have to evaluate 30 or more. This would make a pairwise comparison very difficult due to the excessive number of required comparisons. A similar situation occurs when you are constantly adding or removing alternatives. For example, referring to the previous case, where employees vary in number and must be evaluated semiannually or annually. A pairwise comparison requires a repetitive comparative process every time you add or remove options. This process is tedious. To resolve these two situations (large number of alternatives or frequent addition/removal of alternatives), *ratings models* have been developed (Saaty, 2012). In this approach, criteria priority is still derived by pairwise comparison. Next, a rating scale is specifically developed for each of the criteria and the alternatives are evaluated, independently of each other, using these scales. Let us see how this works.

5.1 Developing Ratings Scales for the Criteria

We begin with the weights (importance) obtained for each criterion (local priorities) in step 2 (Chap. 2) via pairwise comparison. However, instead of comparing the alternatives pairwise, we will develop a rating scale for each of the criteria and the alternatives will be scored against each criterion accordingly. In our previous car example, we had derived the weights for cost (0.669), comfort (0.088), and safety (0.243) as shown in Table 5.1.

E. Mu, M. Pereyra-Rojas, *Practical Decision Making using Super Decisions v3*,
SpringerBriefs in Operations Research, https://doi.org/10.1007/978-3-319-68369-0_5

Table 5.1 Criteria and their weights for the evaluation of alternatives

	Cost	Comfort	Safety
Criteria weights →	0.669	0.088	0.243
Car 1			
Car 2			

Table 5.2 Scale for costs

Cost ($)	Scale	Score
10,000–15,000	Very low	5
16,000–20,000	Low	4
21,000–30,000	Regular	3
31,000–40,000	High	2
>40,000	Very high	1

Table 5.3 Scale for comfort

Comfort	Scale	Score
4 passengers with tight space	Uncomfortable	3
4 passengers with sufficient space	Acceptable	5
4 passengers with large space	Comfortable	7

Table 5.4 Scale for safety

Safety	Scale	Score
Ranked in the 30% inferior percentile	Low	3
Ranked between 31 and 69% percentile	Acceptable	5
Ranked in the 70% superior percentile	High	7

Next, we develop a rating scale for each criterion. This scale can be different for each criterion or the same for all. Examples of scales for each criterion are shown in Tables 5.2, 5.3, and 5.4:

The scales may have different ranges or values for each criterion. A scale with 3, 5, 7, or 10 different values is recommended. The label or tag for each score is also arbitrary and should be selected so as to facilitate the evaluation of alternatives. Finally, take into account that a higher score should reflect greater convenience of the alternative (e.g., a car with higher cost will have a lower score on the scale of Table 5.2).

We now proceed to perform the evaluation of alternatives for each criterion. This assessment can be made with the verbal scales we have created. Let us start with the first row in the rating matrix to rate Car 1 as shown in Table 5.5. For example, with respect to cost, which score should we assign to the Car 1? One possible answer, using the scale of Table 5.2, it could be "Low" as shown in the Car 1-Cost cell in Table 5.5. However, at the moment of performing the calculations, this verbal rating will be replaced by the score 4 (from Table 5.2) as shown in Table 5.6. Similarly, what score should we give to Car 1 with respect to comfort? A possible answer

Table 5.5 Qualitative evaluation of the alternatives

	Cost	Comfort	Safety
Criteria weights →	0.669	0.088	0.243
Car 1	Low	Acceptable	Acceptable
Car 2	High	Comfortable	High

Table 5.6 Quantitative evaluation of the alternatives

	Cost	Comfort	Safety
Criteria weights →	0.669	0.088	0.243
Car 1	4	5	5
Car 2	2	7	7

would be "acceptable" (Table 5.5) which is a "5" for calculation purposes (Table 5.6); and finally, a "High" score is assigned to this alternative regarding safety. Next, we perform a similar evaluation for Car 2 in the second row in the ratings matrix (Table 5.5). In this example, Car 2 has been rated as *High* with respect to cost, *Comfortable* with respect to comfort, and *Acceptable* with respect to safety. Scores can be seen qualitatively or quantitatively as shown in Tables 5.5 and 5.6, respectively.

5.2 Deriving the Overall Priorities (Model Synthesis)

We turn now to the next step to calculate the overall priorities or synthesis which in this case consists in calculating the final scores. The process also consists in calculating the weighted addition of the local priorities as will be shown. We need to multiply each score by the weight of its criteria and add rows for the general priorities or final scores. That is, we calculate the weighted sum of the scores for each alternative for Car 1:

Final score (totals) for Car 1:

$$4 \times 0.669 + 5 \times 0.088 + 5 \times 0.243 = 4.331$$

Final score (totals) for Car 2:

$$2 \times 0.699 + 7 \times 0.088 + 7 \times 0.243 = 3.655$$

To express these totals as overall priorities we simply normalize the totals column; that is, we divide each cell value (4.331 and 3.655, respectively) by the column total (7.986) to obtain the respective priorities for Car 1 (4.331/7.986 = 0.542) and Car 2 (3.655/7.986).

These results are summarized in Table 5.7.

Table 5.7 Overall priorities of the alternatives

	Overall priority	**Totals**	Cost	Comfort	Safety
Criteria weights →			0.669	0.088	0.243
Car 1	**0.542**	**4.331**	4	5	5
Car 2	**0.458**	**3.655**	2	7	7

In other words, Table 5.7 shows that given the importance (weight) that we give to each buying criteria (cost, comfort, and safety), the Car 1 is preferable (0.542 overall priority) to the Car 2 (0.458 overall priority).

5.3 Conclusion

Although final results are not very different from the pairwise comparison analysis we did in a previous chapter (in both cases the Car 1 is the best option), it should be noted that using a ratings model, it would be very easy to assess additional alternatives (e.g., 5 or 6 more cars) by simply adding more rows to the matrix in Table 5.7 and proceed to evaluate them using the developed rating scales. Similarly, withdrawing any car from the list of alternatives would not affect the evaluation made for the others. The reader can imagine the advantage of the ratings method when you consider the effort required to evaluate, for example, 50 vehicles or more. The pairwise comparison would be impractical and the ratings method would be the best option for this type of evaluation.

Reference

Saaty, T. L. (2012). *Decision making for leaders: The analytic hierarchy process for decisions in a complex world* (3rd revised ed.). Pittsburgh: RWS Publications.

Chapter 6
Ratings Models Using Super Decisions v3

Abstract In this chapter, we will learn how to build ratings models using Super Decisions v3. This software version is particularly useful for ratings models. It may be useful to review the theoretical discussion of ratings models in a previous chapter titled "Understanding ratings models." Here we will focus on the how-to aspects of using Super Decisions for ratings models. Readers are encouraged to review the Super Decisions documentation provided by the software developer (http://www.creativedecisions.net).

6.1 Building Ratings Models in Super Decisions

For consistency, we will use the same example of Buying a Car using Super Decisions. The model corresponding to the goal and criteria part is shown in Fig. 6.1. The button is pressed and the goal node "Buying a Car" has been selected to show it is connected to all the criteria in the model. We have not added the alternatives yet because we will do so as part of the ratings model.

First, we will prioritize the criteria (cost, comfort, safety, and aesthetics). This stage follows the same procedure as before.[1] For this purpose, having selected the goal node "Buying a Car," click on the "Judgment" option in the horizontal menu as indicated in Fig. 6.2 and you will obtain the comparison screen.

Click on the appropriate comparison form you want to use. We will use the "questionnaire" format to enter the judgments in our example, as shown in Fig. 6.3. Also, Super Decisions shows the calculated priorities (weights) for each of the criteria in our example. Notice also that inconsistency is less than 0.10 which is acceptable to continue our analysis.

In ratings models, the evaluation of the alternatives (Car 1, Car 2, and Car 3) is not done via pairwise comparison but by rating them with respect to each criterion

[1] In other words, the prioritization of criteria is done via pairwise comparison in both relative and ratings models.

Electronic Supplementary Material The online version of this chapter (https://doi.org/10.1007/978-3-319-68369-0_6) contains supplementary material, which is available to authorized users.

E. Mu, M. Pereyra-Rojas, *Practical Decision Making using Super Decisions v3*, SpringerBriefs in Operations Research, https://doi.org/10.1007/978-3-319-68369-0_6

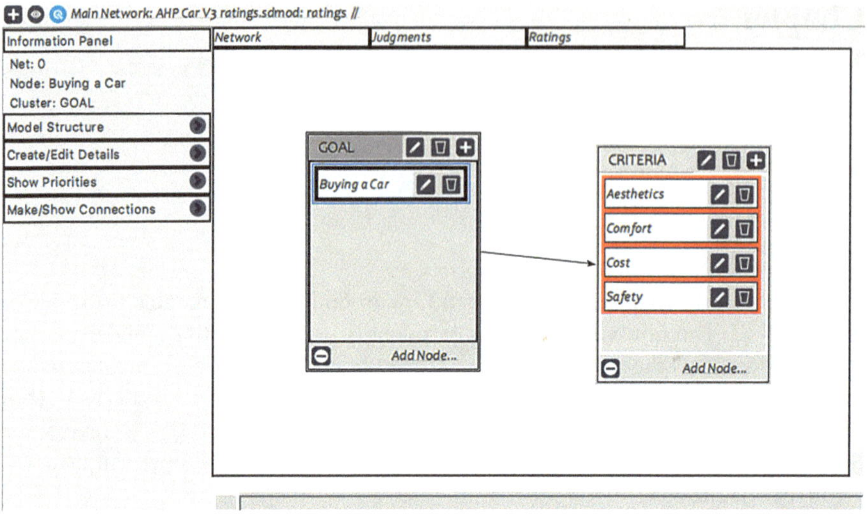

Fig. 6.1 Buying a car criteria model

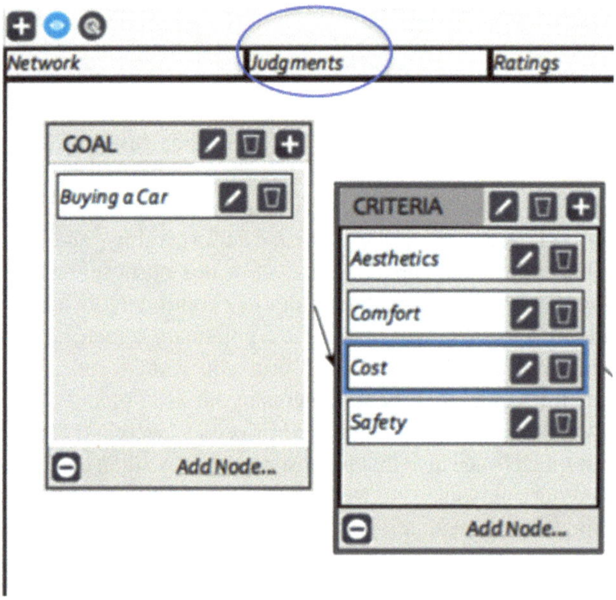

Fig. 6.2 Selecting the "Judgments" option to compare the alternatives

separately.[2] For this purpose, we need to create a ratings scale for each criterion. In

[2] This is the key difference between relative and ratings models. In relative models, the prioritization of alternatives is done via pairwise comparison but in ratings models the prioritization of

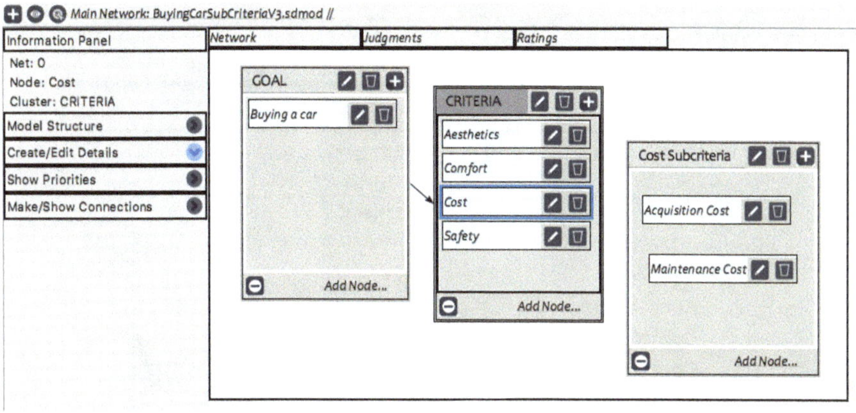

Fig. 6.3 Comparison judgments for the criteria

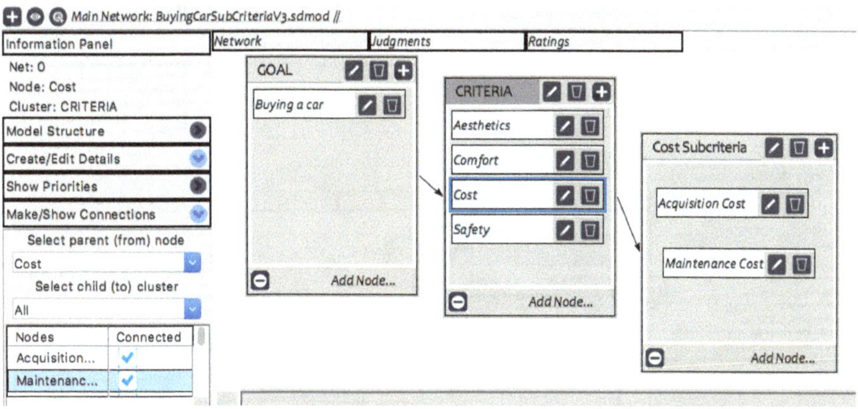

Fig. 6.4 Main window of the ratings method using super decisions

other words, this step requires prioritization of the alternatives according to each of the criteria using their respective ratings scale (we will learn how to create rating scales in a moment); that is, based solely on the criterion *cost*, we need to establish the priority for each alternative using the cost rating scale, then, we repeat the pro-

alternatives is done by rating each alternative using a rating scale (called categories) for each of the criteria.

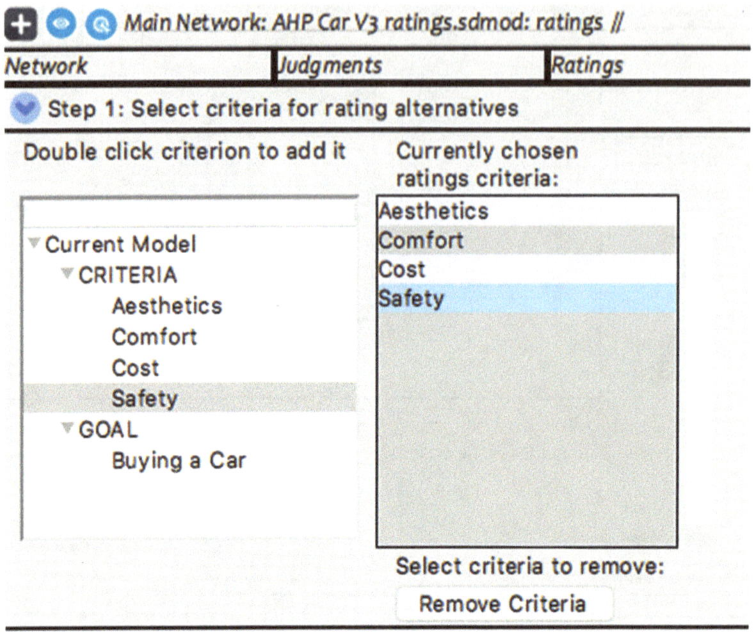

Fig. 6.5 Select criteria window

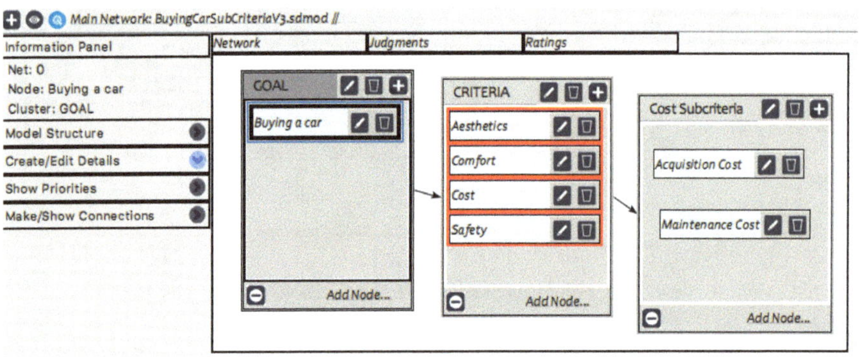

Fig. 6.6 Ratings model with criteria

cess for the criterion *comfort* (using the comfort rating scale) and so on until the alternatives have been rated against all the criteria.

First, we need to create a ratings model. To create a ratings model using Super Decisions v3, select the option "Ratings" from the horizontal bar and you will get the screen shown in Fig. 6.4.

On this screen (Fig. 6.4), select "Step 1: Select criteria for rating alternatives" and you will see the model criteria elements on the left side. Double click on each of criteria to add them to our ratings model. Upon finishing this step you will have the screen shown in Fig. 6.5 (we are showing only a closer view of the upper half of the screen).

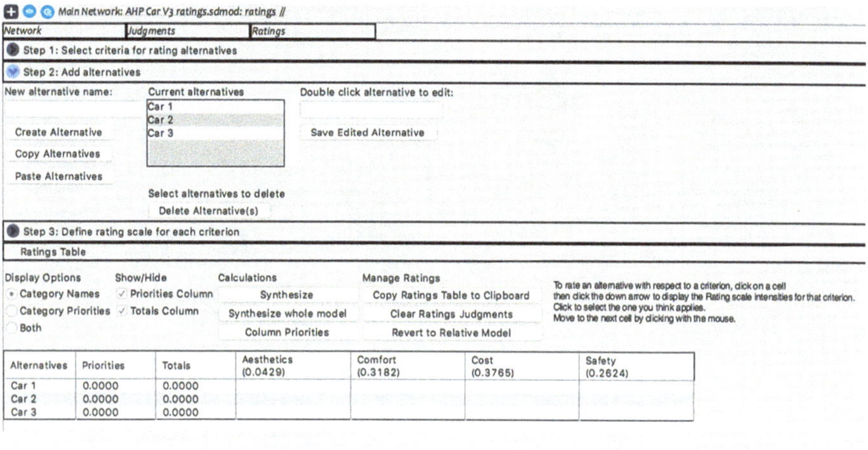

Fig. 6.7 Ratings model with alternatives

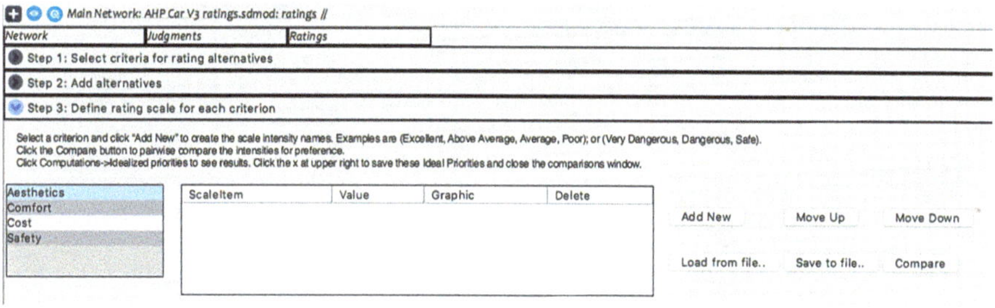

Fig. 6.8 Select criterion to create a rating scale

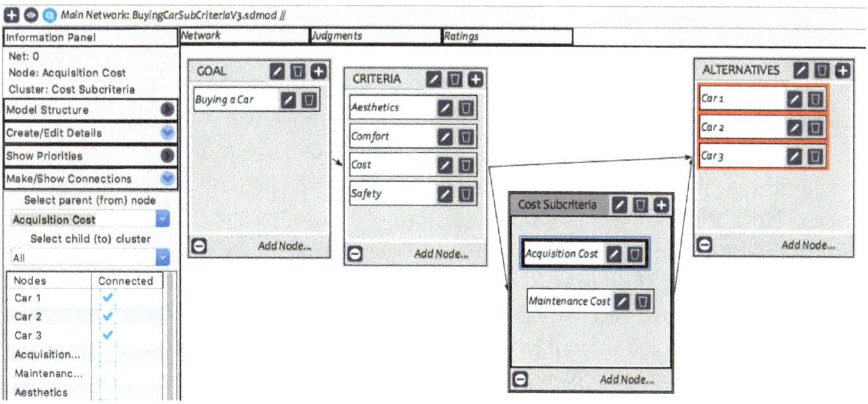

Fig. 6.9 Rating scale creation

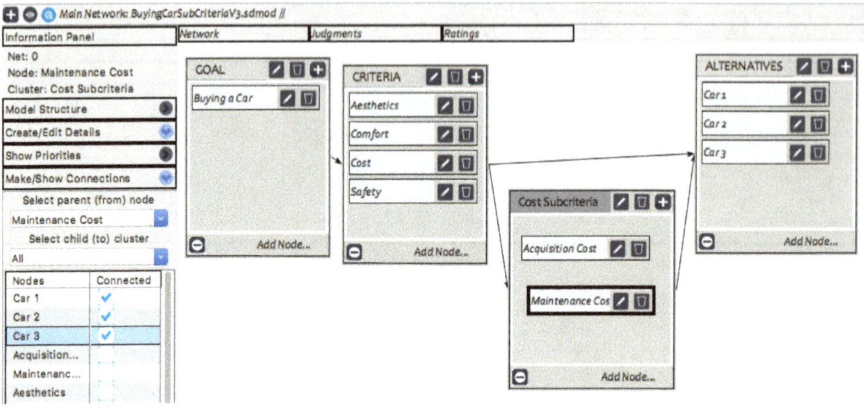

Fig. 6.10 Comparison interface for scale items—questionnaire mode

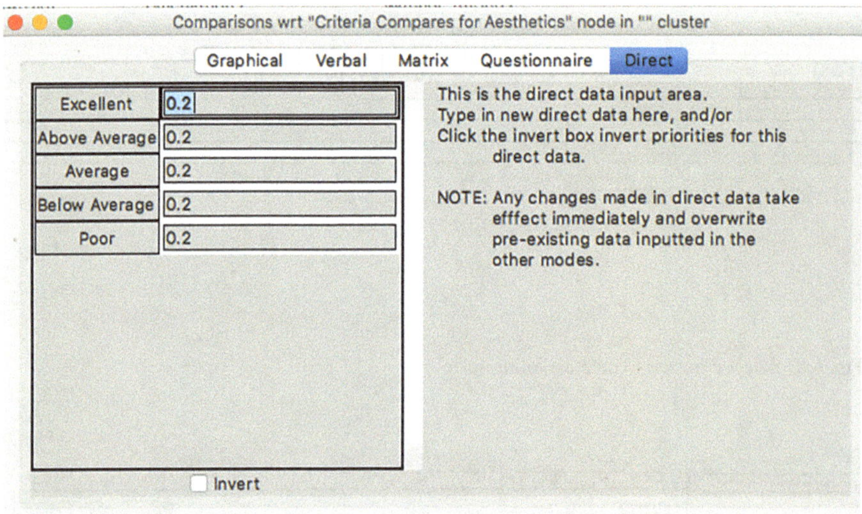

Fig. 6.11 Direct data entry window to enter weights for each scale item

Figure 6.6 shows the "Ratings Table" in the lower half of our ratings model screen. Note that the weights of the criteria (in parenthesis, under the criterion name) are automatically assigned by the software based on the comparison of criteria previously made (Fig. 6.3).

In the next step, we need to add the alternatives. For this, we click on the bar "Step 2: Add alternatives" and we will get a dialog box to enter the alternatives. Enter the first alternative "Car 1" into the "New alternative name" box and click "Create Alternative," do the same for the other two alternatives (Car 2 and Car 3) and upon completion you will have the screen shown in Fig. 6.7. The upper half of this screen shows the "Current Alternatives" while the "Ratings Table" shows Car 1, Car 2, and Car 3 as alternatives in the table (leftmost column in the lower half of the screenshot).

Table 6.1 Values for the scale in our example

Category	Scale	Normal[a]	Ideal[b]
Excellent	5	0.33	1.0
Above average	4	0.27	0.8
Average	3	0.20	0.6
Below average	2	0.13	0.4
Poor	1	0.07	0.2

[a]Calculated by dividing each scale value by the total scale (e.g., 5/15 = 0.33, 5/15 = 0.27)
[b]Calculated by dividing each scale value by the highest value (e.g., 5/5 = 1, 4/5 = 0.8, 3/5 = 0.6)

Now you must create a rating scale for each criterion (cost, comfort, safety, and aesthetics) to assess the alternatives. For this, click on "Step 3: Define rating scale for each criterion" and select the first criterion "Aesthetics" (any selected criterion is highlighted in blue by the software) for which we will create a rating scale as shown in Fig. 6.8.[3]

Next, we will use the "*Add New*" button to enter each of the intensity names: Excellent, Above Average, Average, Below Average, and Poor as shown in Fig. 6.9 (only the upper half of the software screen is shown). We could have used different intensity names if desired and their position can be altered by selecting a name and using the buttons "Move Up" or "Move Down" to change its position in the scale.

Now we need to give a value to each item on the scale. To do that, press the button *Compare* on the rightmost part of the "Step 3" screen (shown in Fig. 6.9) and the software will take you, by default, to compare the rating scale items in a pairwise mode as shown in Fig. 6.10.

We can perform a pairwise comparison to obtain the priorities of each scale item. Another possibility, to be used in this example, is to directly enter the weights for each category. For this, it is necessary to select the Direct tab in the screen shown in Fig. 6.10. The screen shown in Fig. 6.11 is displayed.

If you want to use a 1–5 Likert scale, this can be done by entering the values shown in the "Normal" column in Table 6.1.

The normalized values from this table are entered into the direct comparison window as shown in Fig. 6.12.[4]

By entering these weights in the window shown in Fig. 6.12 we conclude with the weighting of the scale items for the first criterion of Aesthetics. Close this comparison window and we will get back the screen shown in Fig. 6.13 where we can see the scoring values, under the column "Value" automatically calculated to each scale item, based on the weights entered in Fig. 6.12. These scoring values correspond to the ideal column of Table 6.1. These values constitute the ratings values to be used when scoring the alternatives. After verifying that everything is alright with the scale items and values, we are ready to create rating scales for the other criteria.

[3]The rating scale developed for each criterion is called "categories" in previous versions of the Super Decisions software.

[4]After entering the last value, it is always good practice to click on a different cell value to ensure your last value entered was indeed updated by the system.

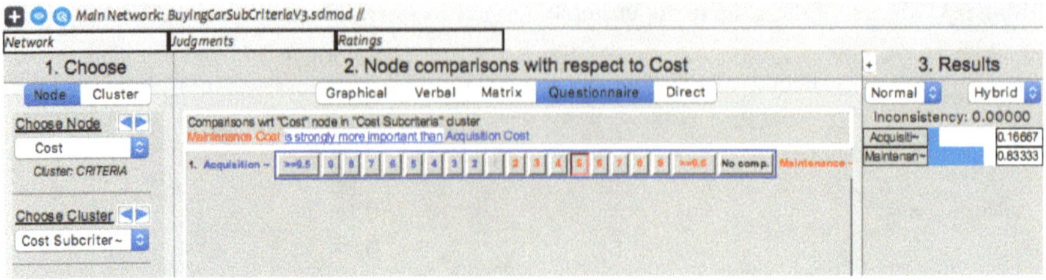

Fig. 6.12 Direct data entry window with weight values for each scale item

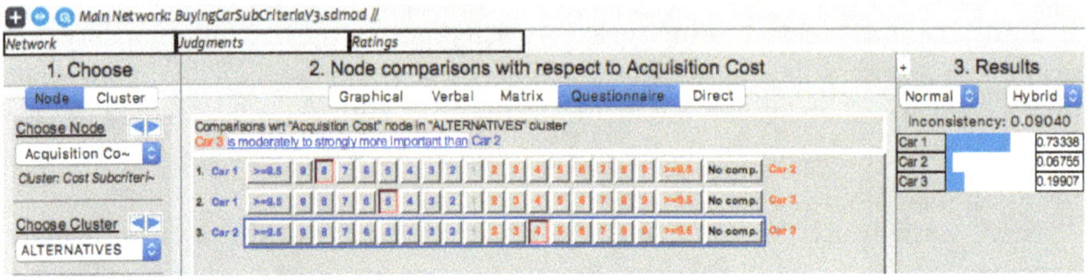

Fig. 6.13 Rating scale values for Aesthetics

Following the same process, we can create categories and different scales for each criterion. However, when there are many criteria it may be more convenient to use the same scale for all categories.

To reuse the same ratings scale we have created for "Aesthetics" for all the other criteria you need to create a template that can be reused later. To do so, make sure to select the criterion whose rating scale you want to use as a template. In our case, this is "Aesthetics" and we must make sure it is selected (we know a criterion is selected because it appears highlighted in light blue as shown for "Aesthetics" in Fig. 6.13). Next, click the button "Save to File" and give a name to the file to be saved. Change the name from "untitled.rcp" to "Likert.rcp" and save it (make sure you save it in the folder you are working with).

Now, we can reuse this template for the other criteria. To do this, let's select the next criterion "Comfort" where we do not have a rating scale yet. Rather than creating a rating scale we will use our template. For this purpose, click on "Load from file" and upload your "Likert.rcp" file previously saved. If done correctly, you will see the same screen shown in Fig. 6.13 except that the selected criterion is "Comfort." Proceed loading the rating scale templates to the other criteria until the four criteria have their corresponding rating scale.

Next, we need to evaluate the alternatives (car 1, car 2, car 3) for each criterion (cost, comfort, aesthetics, and safety) using the rating scales created. For example, to evaluate the Car 1 with respect to the criterion *Aesthetics*, Go to the ratings table and position the cursor in corresponding cell (intersection of row *Car* 1 and Column *Aesthetics*), using the right arrow in the cell, get the drop-down menu with the five categories (excellent, above average, average, etc.) as shown in Fig. 6.14.

Select and click the desired rating, *Average* in our example and this rating will appear now in the corresponding cell. Repeat this procedure until every alternative has been evaluated with respect to each criterion as shown in Fig. 6.15.

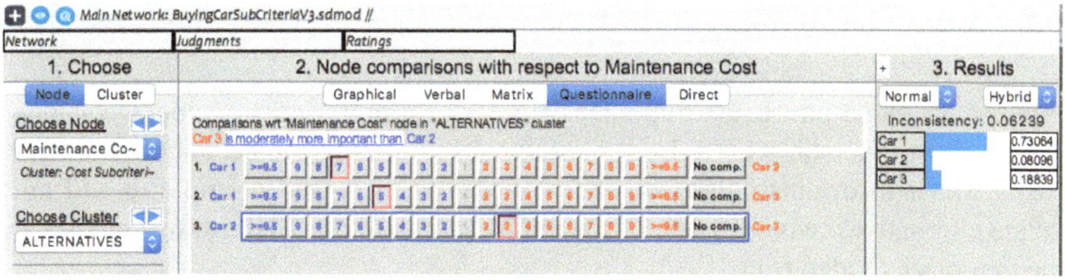

Fig. 6.14 Selecting a rating value to evaluate "Aesthetics"

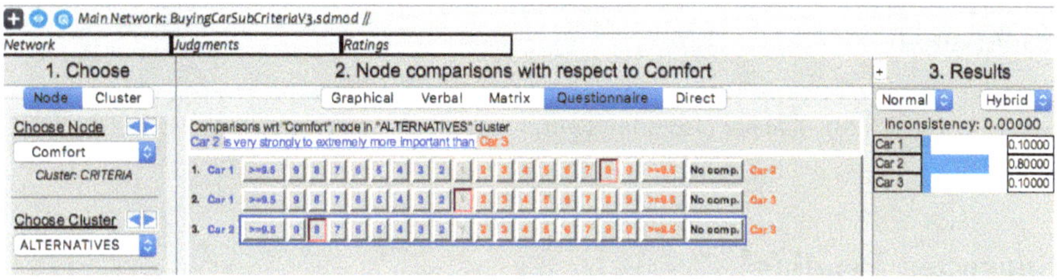

Fig. 6.15 Evaluation of alternatives using the ratings model

Fig. 6.16 Ratings model results in the form of priorities

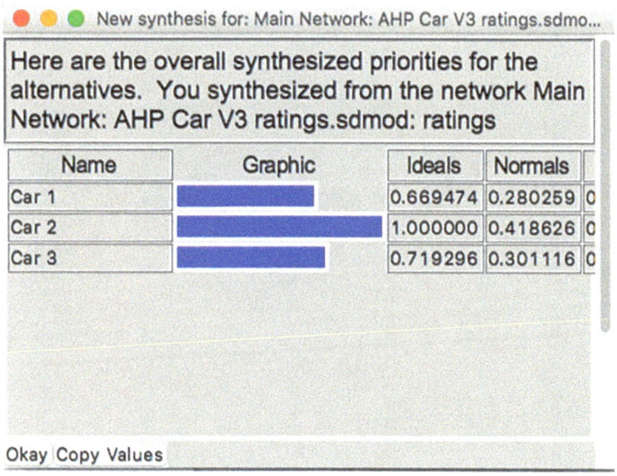

To see the calculated ratings and normalized priorities, make sure that the options "Priorities Columns" and "Totals Column" are checked in the Ratings Table as shown in Fig. 6.15. In Fig. 6.15, the Totals column corresponds to the weighted scoring sum of each alternative. Remember that each verbal rating (e.g., Excellent, Above average) in Fig. 6.15 corresponds to a specific numeric value (e.g., 1, 0.8), also called "Category Priority." You can see these values in the table by selecting "Category Priorities." An alternative that is *Excellent* with respect to every single criterion in the model would get the maximum total score of 1. By normalizing the Totals column (dividing each value by the total addition of the column values) we obtain the Priorities column which shows the relative importance of each alternative. You can also see these results in the traditional way, as priority bars, by selecting *Computations* > *Synthesize* at the top of the Super Decisions menu bar as shown in Fig. 6.16.

6.2 Conclusion

Figure 6.15 shows how to use Super Decisions for Ratings Models (Super Decisions, 2017). Even a person who did not participate in building the decision model can easily use it to evaluate alternatives. Furthermore, it is fairly simple to add and delete alternatives, which is one of the main reasons to use AHP ratings models in the first place (Video 6.1).

Reference

Super Decisions. (2017). *Super Decisions*. Retrieved from http://sdbeta.superdecisions.com

Suggested Reading[5]

Building Ratings Models using Super Decisions v3 https://mix.office.com/watch/1q9cf139gts1n

[5]These videos are the same as those provided in the supplementary material section but the links below are provided as alternative links and for redundancy purposes.

Chapter 7
Benefit/Cost Analysis Using AHP

Abstract In today's world, there are many decisions to be made at every level of management. Learning to closely examine all benefits, opportunities, costs, and risk factors that will affect the decision to launch a project are important skills for decision-makers.

In today's world, there are many decisions to be made at every level of management. Learning to closely examine all benefits, opportunities, costs, and risk factors that will affect the decision to launch a project are important skills for decision-makers (Saaty, 2012). One important problem faced in Benefit/Cost (B/C) analysis is the difficulty involved in assigning a value (monetary perhaps) to benefits, opportunities, costs, and risks. The solution to this problem is to consider both tangible and intangible factors for the benefit/cost assessment process (Wijnmalen, 2007).

7.1 AHP Benefit/Cost Analysis

Traditionally, B/C analysis has been performed to answer the following question: Which alternative will provide the greatest benefits with the lowest costs? Benefits are constituted by gains and pluses of all sorts—Economic, Physical, Psychological, and Social. Similarly, costs are constituted by pains and losses of all sorts.

To perform an AHP B/C analysis, two separate hierarchies (one for benefits and one for costs) must be developed. For the benefits hierarchy, the criteria will be constituted by the expected benefits of the decision. Next, the criteria will be weighted using a pairwise comparison as usual. After this, the alternatives will be prioritized in terms of how beneficial they are. In other words, the comparison questions will always be: With respect to a given criterion, which is the best (most beneficial) alternative?

For the costs hierarchy, the criteria will be constituted by the expected costs of the decision. However, and this is an important consideration, the alternatives are prioritized in terms of how costly they are (i.e., a higher priority reflects a higher cost). For this purpose, the comparison question is: With respect to a given criterion, which alternative is more costly?

E. Mu, M. Pereyra-Rojas, *Practical Decision Making using Super Decisions v3*,
SpringerBriefs in Operations Research, https://doi.org/10.1007/978-3-319-68369-0_7

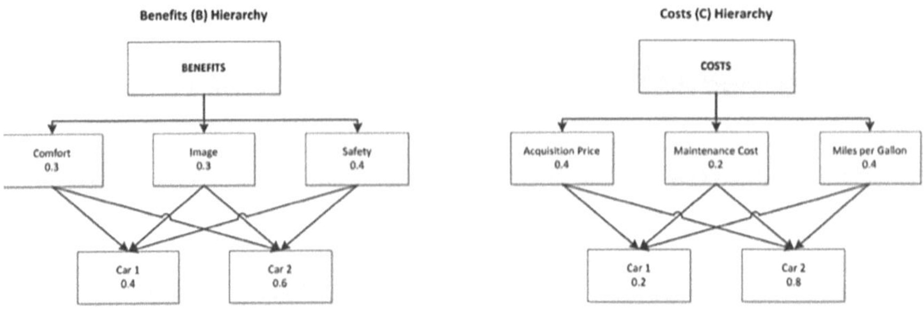

(a) (b)

Altternative	Benefit (B)	Cost (C')	Benefit / Cost	
Car 1	0.4	0.2	2	Best alternative
Car 2	0.6	0.8	0.75	

(c)

Fig. 7.1 AHP B/C analysis. (**a**) The higher the priority of the alternative, the more beneficial (or preferable). (**b**) The higher the priority of the alternative, the more costly (or worse) the alternative. (**c**) The higher the B/C ratio, the more preferable the alternative

Finally, the ratio benefit/cost for the priority of each alternative is computed by dividing the benefit priority by the cost priority of each of the alternatives. The best alternative is the one that has the highest ratio.

To illustrate this with an example, let's assume that we have decided to analyze the decision to purchase a car using a B/C analysis. The steps are as follows:

- Step 1: Build a Benefits Hierarchy, weight the criteria using pairwise comparison, and next prioritize the alternatives based on how beneficial they are (i.e., higher priority indicates higher benefit). Results for the example are shown in Fig. 7.1a.
- Step 2: Build a Cost Hierarchy, weight the criteria using pairwise comparison, and next prioritize the alternatives based on how costly they are (i.e., higher priority indicates higher cost). Results for the example are shown in Fig. 7.1b.
- Step 3: Calculate the B/C ratio for each alternative. The alternative with the highest B/C ratio will be the best. Results for the examples are shown in Fig. 7.1c.

- A more detailed explanation of each example follows.

Step 1: Build a Benefits Hierarchy.

Compare the criteria pairwise to obtain the benefits criteria weights (e.g., "With respect to the benefit expected when buying a car, which criterion is more important: Comfort or Image?" and so on). This procedure is the same as we have done before to determine the relative importance of criteria. As shown in Fig. 7.1a, Safety is the most important criterion (weight: 0.4), followed by Comfort and Image (weight: 0.3 in both cases).

Next, compare the alternatives pairwise with respect to each criterion (i.e., "With respect to Comfort, which alternative is more beneficial: Car 1 or Car 2?" "With respect to Image, which alternative is more beneficial: Car 1 or Car 2?" "With respect to Safety, which alternative is more beneficial: Car 1 or Car 2?"). Finally, calculate the overall priorities.

The benefits hierarchy in Fig. 7.1a shows the final results. According to this, we should purchase the Car 2 which is the most preferable (priority: 0.6) in terms of benefits, with respect to Car 1 (priority: 0.4). However, this would be the right decision if we were only to consider the benefits, but we still need to consider the costs.

Step 2: Build a Cost Hierarchy.

Compare the criteria pairwise to obtain the cost criteria weights (e.g., "With respect to the cost of buying a car, which criterion is more important: Acquisition Cost or Maintenance Cost?" and so on). This procedure is the same as we have done before to determine the relative importance of criteria. As shown in Fig. 7.1b, Maintenance Cost (weight: 0.2) is the least important cost criterion while Acquisition Price and Miles per Gallon consumption are much more important (weight: 0.4 each).

Next, compare the alternatives pairwise with respect to each criterion (i.e., "With respect to Acquisition Price, which alternative is more costly: Car 1 or Car 2?" "With respect to Maintenance Cost, which alternative is more costly: Car 1 or Car 2?" "With respect to Miles per Gallon consumption, which alternative is more costly: Car 1 or Car 2?"). Finally, obtain the overall priorities. The cost hierarchy in Fig. 7.1b shows the final results. According to this, we should purchase the Car 1 which is the least costly (priority: 0.2) with respect to Car 2 (priority: 0.8). However, this would be the right decision if we were only to consider the costs and naturally, wanted to purchase the least costly vehicle. However, in B/C analysis we need to integrate both benefits and costs as shown next.

Step 3: Calculate the B/C Ratio for each Alternative.

To find out which is the best solution, simply divide the benefit by the cost (B/C) for each alternative as shown in the last rightmost column in Fig. 7.1c. The highest B/C ratio is the best alternative, taking into account both benefits and costs. In this case, "Car 1" constitutes the best alternative when taking into account both benefits and costs.

7.2 AHP Benefit*Opportunity/Cost*Risk (BO/CR) Analysis

Traditionally, there are two ways to perform a B/C analysis involving monetary situations: First, it is possible to calculate the ratio Benefit (B) to Costs (C) as B/C. This is called B/C ratio approach. If the benefits are greater than the costs (i.e., ratio $(B/C) > 1$), the project will be profitable. If there are several possible alternatives to choose among, they will be usually prioritized in terms of their B/C ratios from highest to lowest. This is the approach we have used in our previous example.

A second approach is possible based on the net value of the proposed project; that is, if the difference $(B - C)$ is positive (i.e., $(B - C) > 0$), this net value will constitute the net benefit of the project. On the other hand, if this net value is negative, the project will derive losses. Again, if there are several possible alternatives to choose among, they will be prioritized in terms of their net value from highest to lowest.

AHP has extended B/C analysis by allowing mixing tangible (e.g., monetary values) and intangible (e.g., image) considerations. In other words, it is possible to consider various tangible and intangible factors to evaluate the merits, in terms of benefits and costs, of the alternatives (Saaty, 2012).

Also, AHP allows considering opportunities (O) and risks (R) as part of the B/C analysis in what is called BO/CR analysis (Saaty and Ozdemir, 2004). An opportunity is defined as a potential (but not certain) benefit or gain while a risk is defined as a potential (but not certain) cost or loss.

The original proposed formulas that could be considered an extension of the original (B/C) and (B − C) analyses are[1]:

Multiplicative Ratio:

$$(B \times O)/(C \times R)$$

In this expression, it is intuitively noticeable that alternatives with larger numerators (either because B or O are large) and/or smaller denominators (either because C or R are small) will be the most attractive alternatives overall because it will give you the highest ratio. This basically constitutes an extension of the B/C rationale.

Additive with Subtraction:

$$(B + O) - (C + R)$$

The additive with subtraction analysis is an extension of the original net value approach (B − C). This time there are potential benefits (called opportunities) as well as potential costs (called risks). Therefore, the opportunities add to the benefits as well as the risks add to the costs.

In AHP, BOCR analysis is performed as follows: first, a hierarchy is built separately for Benefits (B), Opportunities (O), Costs (C), and Risks (R); second, the alternatives are prioritized with respect to B, O, C, and R in their respective hierarchies and finally, they are combined using either the multiplicative or additive/subtractive formula shown previously. An overview of the process to conduct a BOCR analysis is given in Fig. 7.2.

The multiplicative ratio approach (B * O)/(C * R) can be considered an extension of the well-known B/C ratio analysis previously used. In BO/CR analysis, opportunities refer to potential (but not certain) benefits while risks refer to potential (but not certain) costs as previously indicated. In other words, if a gain is possible but not

[1] For completeness purpose, we should indicate that another proposed formula by Saaty (2012) to integrate BO/CR is the additive/reciprocal: B + O + 1/C + 1/R. However, the use of reciprocals has been strongly questioned by Millet and Schoner (2005), who have argued that taking cost and risk reciprocals actually distorts their originally common scale, thereby producing confounding results. In any case, this formula is rarely used in practice and for this reason is not further discussed in this book.

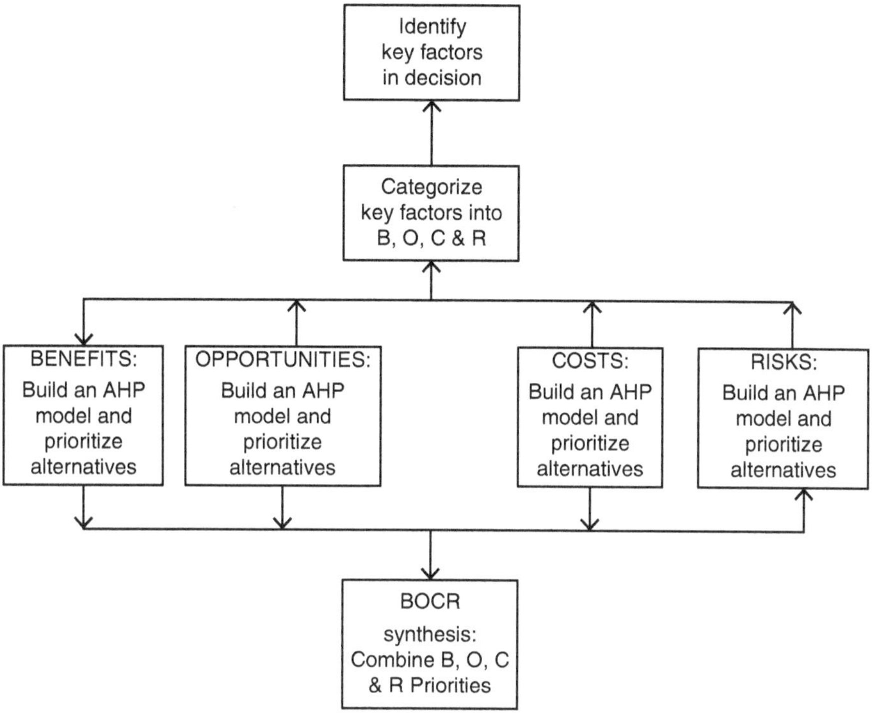

Fig. 7.2 Overview of the BOCR analysis process

certain, it constitutes an opportunity, while if a loss is possible but not certain it constitutes a risk. A simple rule of thumb is typically to ask the question: "Can we be reasonably sure this benefit will occur?" If the answer is "Yes" it is a benefit, if the answer is "No" it is an opportunity. A similar question is made to distinguish costs from risks.

Keep in mind that the priorities of the alternatives in the benefits and opportunities hierarchies reflect how preferable the alternative is (i.e., the higher the priority, the more desirable the alternative is in terms of benefits or opportunities) while the priorities of the alternatives in the costs and risk hierarchies reflect how undesirable the alternative is (i.e., the higher the priority, the more costly or riskier the alternative is). For this purpose, when evaluating the alternatives pairwise with respect to the benefits (or opportunities), the comparison question should be: With respect to this given benefit (or opportunity), which is a better alternative? On the other hand, when evaluating the alternatives pairwise with respect to the costs (or risks), the comparison question should be: With respect to this given criterion, which alternative is more costly (or riskier)?

GOAL Assess University-Uganda University Initiatives from the Perspective of University's School of Education				
CRITERIA	Benefits	Opportunities	Costs	Risks
SUB CRITERIA	Learning Potential 0.163	Interaction w/ Uganda Business 0.088	Training 0.280	Terrorism 0.493
	Mission Sync 0.540	Social Responsibility 0.195	Resources 0.627	Sickness & Disease 0.311
	Recognition 0.297	Project Planning 0.717	Building Renovation & Maintenance 0.094	Accidents & Disasters 0.196
ALTERNATIVES	Bright Kids Uganda	Entebbe School	Children's Rights	End Human Trafficking

	Benefits	Opportunities	Costs	Risks	B/C	B*O/C*R	Ranking
Bright Kids	0.263	0.185	0.334	0.297	1.42	0.885	3
Entebbe School	0.550	0.447	0.458	0.167	1.23	3.297	1
Children's Rights	0.077	0.140	0.096	0.480	0.55	0.161	4
Human Trafficking	0.108	0.225	0.112	0.054	0.48	2.000	2

Fig. 7.3 BO/CR analysis for international opportunities

7.3 A BO/CR Analysis Example

Mu (2016) reports a BO/CR analysis of four proposed university initiatives to collaborate with institutions in Uganda: Bright Kids Uganda, Entebbe School, Children's Rights, and End Human Trafficking. A team of university decision-makers performed a BO/CR analysis from the perspective of the School of Education

(Fig. 7.3, upper half). They created a hierarchy consisting of 4 criteria: Benefits, Opportunities, Costs, and Risks and considered the important decisional factors under each of the criteria. After prioritizing these factors via pairwise comparison, they calculated the local priorities of the alternatives and obtained the overall priorities. As can be seen in Fig. 7.3 (lower half), the Entebbe School initiative was the most convenient in terms of Benefits (Priority: 0.550) and Opportunities (Priority: 0.447). However, this alternative was also the most Costly (Priority: 0.458) but the least Risky (Priority: 0.167). After performing a B * O/C * R calculation of the priorities of the alternatives, it can be seen that the best alternative taking into account benefits, opportunities, costs, and risks is given by Entebbe School which has a BO/CR multiplicative ratio of 3.297, much higher than the other alternatives.

7.4 Conclusion

While BO/CR analysis is very useful for the evaluation of economic alternatives, you must keep in mind some final comments for this type of analysis:

- Do not forget that the comparison questions for alternatives in the cost (risk) hierarchies are the opposite of the questions in the benefits (opportunities) hierarchies. In the benefits (opportunities) hierarchy you select the best (more beneficial or opportunistic) alternative with respect to each criterion but in the cost (riskier) hierarchy you select the worst (more costly) alternative with respect to each criterion.
- Not all the problems can be (or must be) converted to B/C or BO/CR analysis but there are some that are particularly suitable for this type of analysis (e.g., economic decisions).
- Not all the 4 hierarchies are needed. There may be problems suitable for B/C analysis (B/C ratio), B/CR analysis (B/C * R), or similar ones.
- When using Super Decisions or any other software, it may be easier to create and save different AHP models for each of the B, C, O, and R hierarchies and make the corresponding BO/CR ratio calculations outside the software, in a spreadsheet, as shown in our examples.

References

Millet, I., & Schoner, B. (2005). Incorporating negative values into the analytic hierarchy process. *Computers and Operations Research, 32*, 3163–3173.

Mu, E. (2016). Using AHP BOCR analysis for experiential business education and prioritization of international opportunities. *International Journal of Business and Systems Research, 10*(2/3/4), 364–393.

Saaty, T. L. (2012). *Decision making for leaders: The analytic hierarchy process for decisions in a complex world* (3rd revised ed.). Pittsburgh: RWS Publications.

Saaty, T. L., & Ozdemir, M. S. (2004). *The encyclicon: A dictionary of decisions with dependence and feedback based on the analytic network process*. Pittsburgh, PA: RWS Publications.
Wijnmalen, D. J. D. (2007). Analysis of benefits, opportunities, costs, and risks (BOCR) with the AHP–ANP: A critical validation. *Mathematical and Computer Modeling, 46*(7/8), 892–905.

Part III
Advanced

Chapter 8
Group Decision-Making in AHP

Abstract Complex problems usually require the participation of many experts. One reason for this situation is that having more than one opinion on a specific topic may be needed.

Complex problems usually require the participation of many experts. One reason for this situation is that having more than one opinion on a specific topic may be needed (Saaty, 2012). Another reason may be that decisions will affect different stakeholders and for this reason their different perspectives in the decision-making problem are needed (Mu and Stern, 2014). Still another reason to work collaboratively is that complex problems have many different dimensions, each requiring a different kind of expertise. For example, when evaluating large projects for the public, there will be technical, economical, and social considerations to address. AHP is particularly useful for group decision-making, as well as conflict resolution (we will go over this topic in the next chapter), because it is a process which is easy to understand, easy to aggregate different opinions and which allows dividing the overall problem into a set of hierarchies and sub-hierarchies, each of which can be addressed by different experts (Saaty and Peniwati, 2007).

8.1 Working an AHP Model as a Group

As an example, for the decision to select a cloud service provider for the City of Pittsburgh (Mu and Stern, 2014), a top level executive committee determined the five criteria to consider in the decision as well as their importance (weights), as shown in Fig. 8.1. The goal of selecting a cloud service for the City of Pittsburgh (this top goal is not shown but is implicit in Fig. 8.1) and the five criteria identified for this purpose constitutes the main or "big picture" hierarchy for the decision. The key criteria were: Vendor Qualifications, End-User Transparency, Technical Requirements, Financial, and Opportunities. Each of these criteria constitutes a different sub-hierarchy to consider in the decision. A different subcommittee addressed the task of comparing and deriving the weights for each criterion and corresponding sub-criteria. For example, the financial criteria had five sub-criteria: Scope of Services, Distinguishing Compensation, Specific Services, On-Going Preservation,

E. Mu, M. Pereyra-Rojas, *Practical Decision Making*, SpringerBriefs in Operations Research, https://doi.org/10.1007/978-3-319-68369-0_8

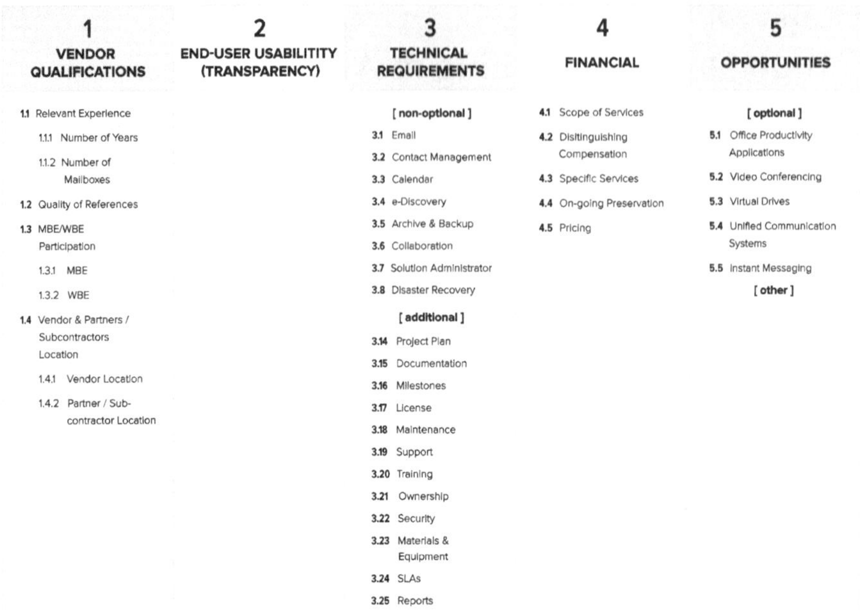

Fig. 8.1 Selecting a cloud service provider for the city of Pittsburgh

and Pricing. This financial sub-hierarchy was evaluated by a subcommittee led by the City Information System's Chief Financial Officer. This is one of the advantages of AHP being able to subdivide the problem into sub-hierarchies that may be addressed by different groups of people. This approach hides the complexity of the problem to the participants who can focus on their specific portion of the problem without losing sight of the big picture.

A project like the one mentioned above may help to understand group decision-making using AHP. An AHP facilitator (AHPF) and a project manager (PM) were assigned to the decision-making process. The first would ensure that all the proper AHP guidelines would be followed and that the meetings were effective (e.g., all participants would have same airtime) while the PM handled all the logistics related to the process (e.g., attendance, minutes, scheduling). Neither the facilitator nor the PM had any voice or vote in the discussions but were present and managed all the evaluation meetings. The project phases were as follows:

First, the top executive committee formed by the CIO, CFO, COO, a user-representative, and an AHP facilitator met to discuss the overall five key criteria (Vendor Qualifications, End-User Usability (Transparency), Technical Requirements, Financial, and Opportunities) and to compare them pairwise[1] to obtain their relative weights in the decision.

[1] The pairwise comparison was done via a printed questionnaire given to each participant. These responses were not visible to the other participants, only to the AHP facilitator and the PM who guaranteed the confidentiality of the responses.

Second, each subcommittee addressed only one of the criterion sub-hierarchy (e.g., the financial subcommittee discussed the financial sub-hierarchy consisting of the criterion "4 Financial" and the five sub-criteria 4.1–4.5 in Fig. 8.1). They discussed the corresponding sub-criteria comparisons and derive their priorities. In a subsequent meeting, each alternative (vendor) was evaluated against their respective criterion. However, this evaluation was preliminary and the participants could take notes if they were not sure about their answers. Their evaluations were based on the vendor proposals delivered to the City in response to the request for proposals.

Third, each vendor was given the opportunity to present live their proposals and to address questions raised by the evaluating subcommittees. After each vendor presentation, a meeting would take place to discuss once more the merits of each vendor. Each criteria sub-hierarchy was discussed and evaluated only by the specific committee. Participants would turn in their questionnaires, this time with the final comparison judgments which were aggregated into a single questionnaire by the AHP facilitator.

8.1.1 About the Meetings

Although a comprehensive discussion of how to conduct AHP meetings is beyond the scope of this book, there are some important considerations to keep in mind:

- *Meeting Duration*: Meetings ranged between 1 and 2 h. However, the duration of the meeting was specified before hand so participantscould allocate the proper time to this process.
- *Meeting Objective*: Participants were clearly told in advance what the objective of the meeting was.
- *Participant Airtime*: To ensure that all participants would have the same airtime, the facilitator would make sure that each participant was given the opportunity to speak by following a sequential order to give the word to the meeting participants. Participants had 3 min each to argue their thoughts.
- *Deciding How To Decide*[2]: It was agreed that for each meeting, the facilitator would explain the situation, and objective of the meeting. Next, each participant would have a 3-min time slot to present his/her argument. After this, the facilitator would summarize the different arguments and a second round of 3 min was given to each participant to counterargue or reinforce judgments. Next, each participant would mark their comparison judgments on a paper questionnaire. At the end of the meeting, the AHPF would collect the questionnaires to aggregate the judgments.

[2] *Deciding How to Decide* is a term coined by Roberto (2005) and highlights the idea that teams must agree to the decision-making process before getting involved in the decision itself. This ensures that whatever decision is reached by the participants, it will be considered fair and taking into account all the different positions. In general, the success of the group decision-making using AHP will depend on the effectiveness of managing the group dynamics and standard methods for effective team management (Forsyth 2013; Roberto 2005).

8.2 Aggregation of Judgments Using a Spreadsheet

When performing pairwise comparisons, each participant may have a different opinion about the proper preference (i.e., which element is more important than the other) and the intensity of that preference.

The rule for aggregation of judgments in a comparison matrix is very simple: Combine the judgments using the geometric mean. The geometric mean of two intensities intensity 1 (I1) and intensity 2 (I2) is the square root of their product. The geometric mean of three intensities I1, I2, and I3 is the cubic root of their product and so forth.

This is much easier to understand with an example. Also, for convenience, we will show again Saaty's comparison 1–9 scale used to quantify verbal judgments, as shown in Table 8.1.

Let us assume that three decision-makers (DM1, DM2, and DM3), while judging the importance of the criterion "Cost" versus "Comfort" with respect to the goal of buying a car, have made the following judgments[3]:

Decision-Maker 1 Judgment DM1: **Comfort** is from "*Very Strongly* more important (7)" to "*Extremely* important (9)" with respect to **Cost**.

When working with a spreadsheet, this judgment means we must enter (using the scale from Table 8.1) the intensity value 8 in the cell Comfort (row)-Cost (column) as shown in Table 8.2. Notice that by doing this, the comparison Cost (row)-Comfort (column) will be the reciprocal value of 1/8.

Decision-Maker 2 Judgment DM2: **Comfort** is from "*Moderately* more important (3)" to "*Strongly* more important (5)" with respect to **Cost**.

The second decision-maker also thinks that Comfort is more important than Cost but disagrees in the intensity and judges it to be 4 (from the scale in Table 8.1) as shown in Table 8.3. Again, the reciprocal comparison becomes 1/4.

Decision-Maker 3 Judgment DM3: **Cost** is from "*Moderately* more important (3)" to "*Strongly* more important (5)" with respect to **Comfort**.

Table 8.1 Saaty's comparison scale

Verbal judgment	Numeric value
Extremely more important	9
	8
Very strongly more important	7
	6
Strongly more important	5
	4
Moderately more important	3
	2
Equally important	1

[3] These DMs may have recorded their judgments in 3 different comparison matrices. You need to aggregate the judgments manually and enter the result into a new aggregate matrix.

Table 8.2 DM1 comparison judgment of comfort versus cost

Buying a car	Comfort	Cost	Safety
Comfort		**8**	
Cost	1/8		
Safety			

Table 8.3 DM2 comparison judgment of comfort versus cost

Buying a car	Comfort	Cost	Safety
Comfort		**4**	
Cost	1/4		
Safety			

Table 8.4 DM3 comparison judgment for comfort versus cost

Buying a car	Comfort	Cost	Safety
Comfort		**1/4**	
Cost	4		
Safety			

This decision-maker differs much more from the others because DM3 considers that Cost rather than Comfort is more important. The intensity value for Cost (with respect to Comfort) is 4. This means that the intensity value entered for the comparison in the Comfort (row)-Cost (column) cell should be 1/4 (Comfort/Cost = 1/4). Following the convention of using red font when the column is more important than the row, the cell comfort-cost has the value **1/4** as shown in Table 8.4. This means that the reciprocal comparison Cost (row)-Comfort (column) will be 4/1 = 4 (Cost/Comfort = 4) as shown in Table 8.4.

8.3 Aggregation of Judgments in a Comparison Matrix

To aggregate these three judgments we calculate the geometric mean of these three values; that is, we calculate the cubic root (because there are three DMs) of their intensity product:

$$\text{Aggregated DM} = \text{Cubic Root of} \left(8 \times 4 \times 1/4\right) = \text{Cubic Root of } 8 = 2.$$

Therefore, we enter 2 in the cell comfort-cost in Table 8.5.

Notice that if we would have started the aggregation using the cell cost-comfort (instead of comfort-cost), the result of calculating the geometric mean of the judgments provided by DM1, DM2, and DM3 would be:

$$1/\left[\text{Cubic Root of} \left(8 \times 4 \times 1/4\right)\right] = 1/2$$

Table 8.5 Aggregated judgments for DM1, DM2, and DM3

Buying a car	Comfort	Cost	Safety
Comfort		**2**	
Cost			
Safety			

Table 8.6 Aggregated judgments for DM1, DM2, and DM3, with reciprocal comparison

Buying a car	Comfort	Cost	Safety
Comfort		**2**	
Cost	1/2		
Safety			

which is the expected value for the aggregated cell cost-comfort (cost/comfort), given that the Comfort-Cost (Comfort/Cost) value is 2. This property of reciprocity does not hold if we were to use the arithmetic mean for the aggregation of the judgments. This demonstrates that the geometric mean is the correct way to aggregate judgments in AHP and the geometric mean aggregation for our cell comparison example is shown in Table 8.6.

8.4 Aggregation of Judgments Using Super Decisions

Let us assume that three decision-makers (DM1, DM2, and DM3), when judging the importance of the criterion "Comfort" versus "Cost" with respect to the goal of buying a car, have made the following judgments[4] using *Super Decisions* in questionnaire mode[5]:

DM1: **Comfort** is from *Very Strongly to Extremely* more important with respect to **Cost** (Table 8.7).

DM2: **Comfort** is from *Moderately to Strongly* more important with respect to **Cost** (Table 8.8).

DM3: **Cost** is from *Moderately to Strongly* more important with respect to **Comfort** (Table 8.9).

Notice that both DM1 and DM2 consider that Comfort is more important than Cost with an intensity of 8 and 4, respectively. However, DM3 thinks differently since, in this case, Cost is perceived more important than Comfort with an intensity of 4. Mathematically, these judgments can be represented as:

DM1: Comfort/Cost = 8.

DM2: Comfort/Cost = 4.

DM3: Comfort/Cost = 1/4.

[4] For simplicity, we will use the same values from our previous example.

[5] These DMs may have recorded their judgments in 3 different *Super Decisions* models or in 3 different paper questionnaires. You need to aggregate the judgments manually and enter the result into a new comparison questionnaire in *Super Decisions*.

Table 8.7 Questionnaire judgment for decision-maker 1

Comfort	9	8	7	6	5	4	3	2	1	2	3	4	5	6	7	8	9	Cost

Table 8.8 Questionnaire judgment for decision-maker 2

Comfort	9	8	7	6	5	4	3	2	1	2	3	4	5	6	7	8	9	Cost

Table 8.9 Questionnaire judgment for decision-maker 3

Comfort	9	8	7	6	5	4	3	2	1	2	3	4	5	6	7	8	9	Cost

Table 8.10 Questionnaire aggregate judgment

Comfort	9	8	7	6	5	4	3	**2**	1	2	3	4	5	6	7	8	9	Cost

To aggregate these three judgments we calculate the geometric mean of these three values; that is, we calculate the cubic root (because there are 3 DMs) of their intensity product; that is:

$$\text{Aggregated DM} = \text{Cubic Root of}\left(8 \times 4 \times 1/4\right) = \text{Cubic Root of } 8 = 2.$$

What if the aggregate result is not an integer but a decimal number? (Table 8.10) In questionnaire mode, we would need to use the closest integer value. However, the easiest way to handle decimal aggregations is to enter them in matrix mode, making sure that the arrow in the matrix points to the dominant element (Column Cost in our final result).[6] For example, assuming that we would have obtained an aggregate value of 2.5 for the aggregate judgment of Cost versus Comfort, it would be recorded as shown in Fig. 8.2. Matrix mode is capable of managing decimals for the intensity values.

8.5 Consistency in Group Judgments

There are two ways to address consistency problems in group decision-making: the first way is to go back to the inconsistent decision-makers and work with them in adjusting their judgments. However, this is not always possible if the comparison judgments are anonymous or the respondents are not present. A second way consists in using only the minimum number of comparisons to avoid redundant questions leading to inconsistency. The minimum number of questions is comprised of only the comparison judgments in the diagonal above the main diagonal (highlighted in Table 8.11—C1/C2; C2/C3; C3/C4; C4/C5; C5/C6; C6/C7) of the comparison matrix. Using this minimum number of comparison questions, we can reproduce

[6] To change the direction of the arrow, simply click on the arrow and it will point either to the row (changing to blue color) or to the column (changing to red color), respectively.

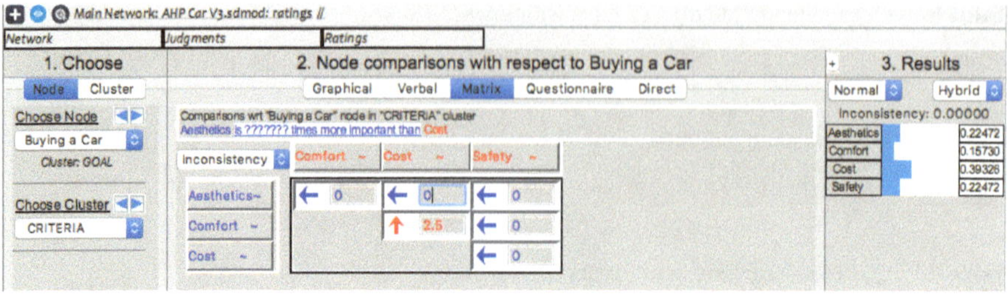

Fig. 8.2 Aggregate judgment in matrix mode

Table 8.11 Minimizing the number of comparisons

	C1	C2	C3	C4	C5	C6	C7
C1	**1**	C1/C2					
C2		**1**	C2/C3			**Upper part**	
C3			**1**	C3/C4			
C4				**1**	C4/C5		
C5		**Lower part**			**1**	C5/C6	
C6						**1**	C6/C7
C7							**1**

what all the other matrix judgments would be (upper part of the matrix) in the case of perfect consistency, as shown in Table 8.11.

The minimum number of comparisons required for a matrix 7 × 7 as the one shown in the above figure is provided by the diagonal (shaded) above the unit diagonal (filled with 1 s). Once we have these comparisons, the rest of comparison judgments in the upper part of the matrix can be calculated. As an example, to calculate the comparison C1/C3 (the intersection of row C1 and column C3 in the example matrix), we do the following calculation: (C1/C2) * (C2/C3) = C1/C3. We can repeat the same process for the rest of cells in the upper part of the matrix. The values in the lower part of the matrix are simply the reciprocal from the upper part. For example, the value for the comparison C3/C1 (the intersection of row C3 and column C1 in the lower part of the matrix) will be the reciprocal of the value C1/C3 in the upper part of the matrix.

8.6 Conclusion

As you can see, aggregating the judgments of individual decision-makers is relatively straightforward. Furthermore, the judgment collection can be done for each decision-maker separately; that is, it does not need to be done simultaneously for all of them. The use of AHP for group decision-making (Saaty and Peniwati, 2007) and conflict resolution (Saaty and Alexander, 2013) has been widely documented in different settings.

References

Forsyth, D. R. (2013). *Group dynamics* (6th ed.). Belmont: Wadsworth Publishing.

Mu, E., & Stern, H. (2014). The City of Pittsburgh goes to the cloud: A case study of cloud strategic selection and deployment. *Journal of Information Technology Teaching Cases, 4*, 70–85.

Roberto, M. A. (2005). *Why great leaders don't take yes for an answer: Managing for conflict and consensus* (1st ed.). FT Press.

Saaty, T. L. (2012). *Decision making for leaders: The analytic hierarchy process for decisions in a complex world* (3rd revised ed.). Pittsburgh: RWS Publications.

Saaty, T. L., & Alexander, J. M. (2013). *Conflict resolution: The analytic hierarchy approach.* Pittsburgh, PA: RWS Publications.

Saaty, T. L., & Peniwati, K. (2007). *Group decision-making: Drawing out and reconciling differences*. Pittsburgh, PA: RWS Publications.

Chapter 9
AHP for Group Negotiation and Conflict Resolution

Abstract AHP has been widely used for group negotiation and conflict resolution [Saaty and Alexander. (2013). *Conflict resolution: The analytic hierarchy approach.* Pittsburgh, PA: RWS Publications].

9.1 Introduction

AHP has been widely used for group negotiation and conflict resolution (Saaty, 2012; Saaty & Alexander, 2013). A hierarchy consisting of a decision goal, criteria (objectives[1]), and alternatives constitutes an actor's vision of the world. In many cases, the different actors agree to the decision goal and the possible alternatives (first and third levels on the hierarchy); however, the final decision is difficult to reach because they have different criteria (objectives) when making the decision (second level on the hierarchy).

9.2 Essentials of AHP Negotiation

As an example, consider the hostage situation analyzed by Saaty and Mu (1997). This situation was modeled as a typical 3-level hierarchy: goal, objectives (criteria), and actions (alternatives).

Situation: Guerrilla members from the revolutionary movement Tupac Amaru (MRTA) had taken hostages and demanded the liberation of their jailed comrades by the Peruvian government. On the other hand, the government had been elected for its success in combating guerrillas and imprisoning their leaders.

The decision (goal) was clearly the same (to end the crisis successfully) for both the government and the guerrillas (Top level goal in Figs. 9.1 and 9.2).

The objectives (criteria) in this crisis were clearly distinct for both the MRTA and the government. For example, while the government wanted to save its image, save hostage lives, and prevent terrorism altogether (level 2 in Fig. 9.1), the MRTA

[1] Decision-making criteria are also referred as decision-making objectives as will be seen in this chapter.

E. Mu, M. Pereyra-Rojas, *Practical Decision Making using Super Decisions v3*, SpringerBriefs in Operations Research, https://doi.org/10.1007/978-3-319-68369-0_9

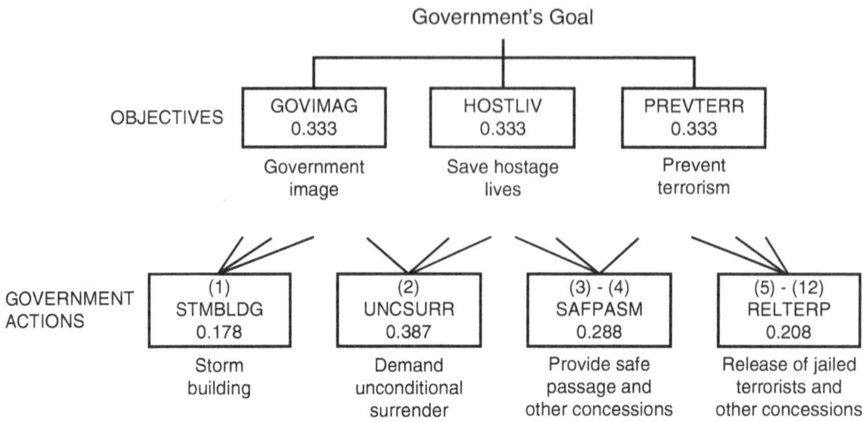

Fig. 9.1 Government's perspective for the decision

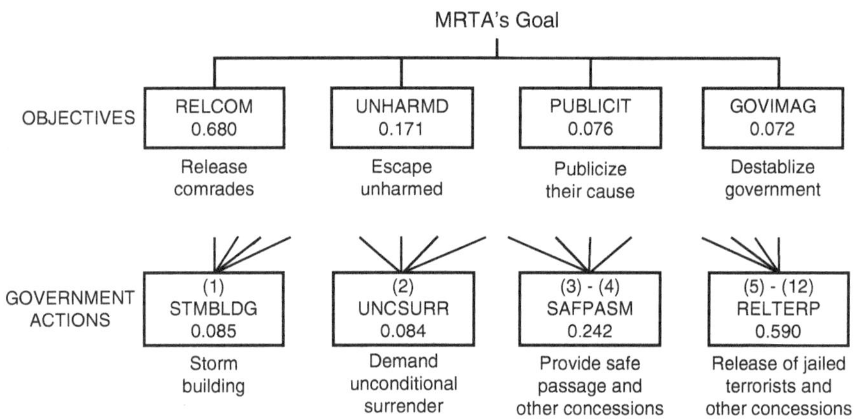

Fig. 9.2 MRTA's perspective for the decision

wanted the release of their jailed comrades and escape unharmed while publicizing their cause and destabilizing the government (middle level in Fig. 9.2).

The actions were also clear. In principle, they ranged from storming the building and demanding unconditional surrender to the release of jailed terrorists and other concessions (lowest level in Figs. 9.1 and 9.2).

Figures 9.1 and 9.2 show the decision as seen by the government and the MRTA, respectively, as reported in Saaty and Mu (1997).

The concept of negotiation involves, in principle, looking for a solution that can be beneficial to both parties. Furthermore, the main goal in public policy is to maximize the common good rather than any party's in particular. If we adopt this approach for the search of a compromised solution, then the best solution should be the one that maximizes the value of the alternatives for both parties. This analysis can be seen in Table 9.1. This table shows the AHP analysis for the government and

Table 9.1 Combining the government and MRTA's perspectives

Government's perspective		MRTA's perspectives		Combined perspectives
Key objectives	Priority	Key objectives	Priority	
		RELCOM	0.680	
GOVIMAG	0.333	UNHARMD	0.171	
HOSTLIVE	0.333	PUBLICIT	0.076	
PREVTERR	0.333	GOVIMAG	0.072	
Potential government actions				Product of the two vectors for compromise:
UNCSURR	0.387 (1)	UNCSURR	0.084 (4)	0.387 × 0.084 = 0.03
SAFPASM	0.288 (2)	SAFPASM	0.242 (2)	0.288 × 0.242 = 0.07
RELTERP	0.208 (3)	RELTERP	0.590 (1)	**0.208 × 0.590 = 0.12**
STMBLDG	0.178 (4)	STMBLDG	0.085 (3)	0.178 × 0.085 = 0.02

MRTA's perspective separately. For the government, it has been considered that all their objectives have the same weight (0.333 each). For the MRTA, the release of their jailed comrades had the greatest value (0.680) since this was the reason for their armed incursion.

Table 9.1 shows that for the government, the preferred alternative would be to demand unconditional surrender (UNCSURR: 0.387) followed by providing safe passage to the guerrillas (SAFPSM: 0.288) and the worst case scenario would be storming into the building (STMBLDG: 0.178) due to the expected loss of hostage lives. On the other hand, for the MRTA's members, the best possible alternative would be a negotiated release of jailed comrades (RELTERP: 0.590) followed by safe passage (SAFPASM: 0.242) and quite distantly by UNCSURR and STMBLDG.

Which would be the best compromised solution that would maximize the priorities given to the alternatives by both parties? To do this, we multiply the priorities given to each alternative by each party, as shown in Table 9.1. The highest compromise product is obtained by the RELTERP alternative (0.208 × 0.590 = 0.12) and therefore, constitutes the best compromised solution if our overall approach is maximizing the overall value for the parties.[2]

[2] The objective of this exposition is only to show how to combine different perspectives. The reader is referred to the original Saaty and Mu (1997)'s reference if interested in the specific analysis of this hostage situation.

Table 9.2 Aggregation of school perspectives for B, O, C, and R.

Benefits					
Perspectives:	School of education	School of nursing	School of psychology	Aggregation of B perspectives	
	Be	Bn	Bp	B	**B**
Alternatives				(Be*Bn*Bp)	**Normal**
Bright kids	0.263	0.427	0.12	0.013	0.169
Entebbe school	0.55	0.233	0.45	0.058	0.723
Children's rights	0.077	0.076	0.16	0.001	0.012
Human trafficking	0.108	0.263	0.27	0.008	0.096
Opportunities					
Perspectives:	School of education	School of nursing	School of psychology	Aggregation of O perspectives	
	Oe	On	Op	O	**O**
Alternatives				(Oe*On*Op)	**Normal**
Bright kids	0.185	0.513	0.14	0.013	0.345
Entebbe school	0.447	0.055	0.55	0.014	0.351
Children's rights	0.14	0.249	0.08	0.003	0.072
Human trafficking	0.225	0.173	0.23	0.009	0.232
Costs					
Perspectives:	School of education	School of nursing	School of psychology	Aggregation of C perspectives	
	Ce	Cn	Cp	C	**C**
Alternatives				(Ce*Cn*Cp)	**Normal**
Bright kids	0.334	0.501	0.24	0.040	0.453
Entebbe school	0.458	0.243	0.4	0.045	0.503
Children's rights	0.096	0.21	0.14	0.003	0.032
Human trafficking	0.112	0.045	0.21	0.001	0.012
Risks					
Perspectives:	School of education	School of nursing	School of psychology	Aggregation of R perspectives	
	Re	Rn	Rp	R	**R**
Alternatives				(Re*Rn*Rp)	**Normal**
Bright kids	0.297	0.323	0.23	0.022	0.406
Entebbe school	0.167	0.066	0.13	0.001	0.026
Children's rights	0.48	0.146	0.33	0.023	0.425
Human trafficking	0.054	0.465	0.31	0.008	0.143

9.3 AHP Negotiation in BOCR Models

It is possible to extend the above concepts to the case of benefits/opportunities/cost/risk (BOCR) analysis (Mu, 2016). Table 9.2 reports a BOCR analysis for four possible international initiatives (alternatives): Bright Kids, Entebbe School, Children's Rights, and Human Trafficking. These opportunities for international collaboration were discussed from the perspective of three different schools (stakeholders) at a

Table 9.3 BO/CR analysis of the aggregated perspectives

	B	O	C	R	B*O/C*R	BO/CR Normal	Rank
Bright kids	0.169	0.345	0.453	0.406	0.317	0.010	3
Entebbe school	0.723	0.351	0.503	0.026	19.159	**0.588**	**1**
Children's rights	0.012	0.072	0.032	0.425	0.063	0.002	4
Human trafficking	0.096	0.232	0.012	0.143	13.061	0.401	2

liberal arts university: School of Education, School of Nursing, and School of Psychology. Obviously, the benefit provided by each initiative to each of the schools is different. For example, the priority given to the Bright Kids alternative by each school was 0.263, 0.427, and 0.12, respectively (Benefits results in Table 9.2). The product aggregation and normalization[3] of the three school perspectives is shown in the rightmost column (B Normal) in Table 9.2. This same process is done for each alternative in the benefits, opportunities, costs, and risks analysis (B Normal, O Normal, C Normal, and R Normal) as shown in Table 9.2. Finally, to calculate the best overall alternative taking into account B, O, C, and R considerations, the formula (B * O)/(C * R) is used, as shown in Table 9.3. As an example, for the Entebbe School alternative (second row in Table 9.3), this formula is calculated as (0.723 * 0.351)/(0.503 * 0.026) leading to the value 19.59 which is by far the highest result with respect to the other alternatives. We can normalize these results to conclude that the best overall alternative (Rank = 1) is the Entebbe School initiative with 0.588 of the overall preference, followed by Human Trafficking (Rank = 2) with 0.401.

9.4 Conclusion

In this chapter, you have learned how to negotiate different parties' perspectives by integrating their hierarchy or BOCR perspectives. One important advantage of using AHP for negotiation and conflict resolution is that the parties do not need to come together to discuss the problem. Each hierarchy can be discussed separately with each of the parties by the facilitator. This comes very handy when it is not possible to get the parties together due to practical reasons.

[3] The reader may remember that the normalization values are obtained by adding all the values in a given column and dividing each value by the total sum. For example, B Normal for the Entebbe School alternative (0.723)—in the Benefits hierarchy in Table 9.2—was obtained by adding all the values in the previous column (0.013 + 0.058 + 0.001 + 0.008) and next dividing the Entebbe School aggregated value (0.058) by this sum.

References

Mu, E. (2016). Using AHP BOCR analysis for experiential business education and prioritization of international opportunities. *International Journal of Business and Systems Research, 10*(2–4), 364–393. https://doi.org/10.1504/IJBSR.2016.075749.

Saaty, T. L. (2012). *Decision making for leaders: The analytic hierarchy process for decisions in a complex world* (3rd revised ed.). Pittsburgh: RWS Publications.

Saaty, T. L., & Alexander, J. M. (2013). *Conflict resolution: The analytic hierarchy approach.* Pittsburgh, PA: RWS Publications.

Saaty, T. L., & Mu, E. (1997). The Peruvian hostage crisis of 1996–1997: What should the government do? *Socio-Economic Planning Sciences, 31*(3), 165–172.

Chapter 10
Application Examples

Abstract We have reached the end of this introduction to the Analytic Hierarchy Process. You already know all the key building elements to start using AHP in many different applications. We would like to take advantage of this last chapter to show some examples of AHP applications in the expectations that they will allow you to reflect on what you have learned so far.

We have reached the end of this introduction to the Analytic Hierarchy Process. You already know all the key building elements to start using AHP in many different applications. We would like to take advantage of this last chapter to show some examples of AHP applications in the expectations that they will allow you to reflect on what you have learned so far.

10.1 AHP Handling of Stakeholders

The most classic AHP application is the selection of a single best alternative among several ones. This is how all newcomers to AHP learn the method. In our case, we started selecting the best car to buy. However, applications in practice tend to be far more complicated.

Mu et al. (2012) report on the selection of a new generation of electronic portfolios for a higher learning institution. An electronic portfolio is a web-based application used by students to showcase their projects and academic progress to students, faculty, administrators, and potential employers. Furthermore, faculty values the use of electronic portfolios because it simplifies the submission and grading of projects. Finally, higher-education administrators are interested in electronic portfolios because it facilitates the documentation of students' academic progress for accreditation purposes. While the key functionalities of an electronic portfolio, to be used for selection purposes, can be identified, the importance or weight attributed to each of these characteristics will depend on the specific stakeholder: students, faculty, or administrators.

An *ad hoc* committee identified the key characteristics (decision criteria) of electronic portfolios and then requested students, faculty, and administrators to derive

E. Mu, M. Pereyra-Rojas, *Practical Decision Making using Super Decisions v3*, SpringerBriefs in Operations Research, https://doi.org/10.1007/978-3-319-68369-0_10

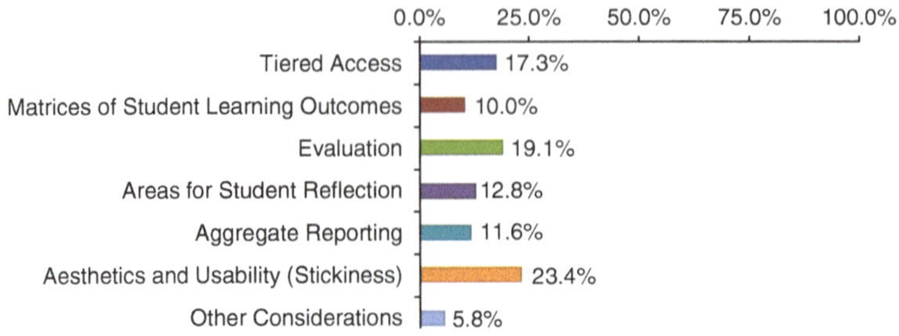

Fig. 10.1 Faculty perspective ePortfolio selection criteria weights

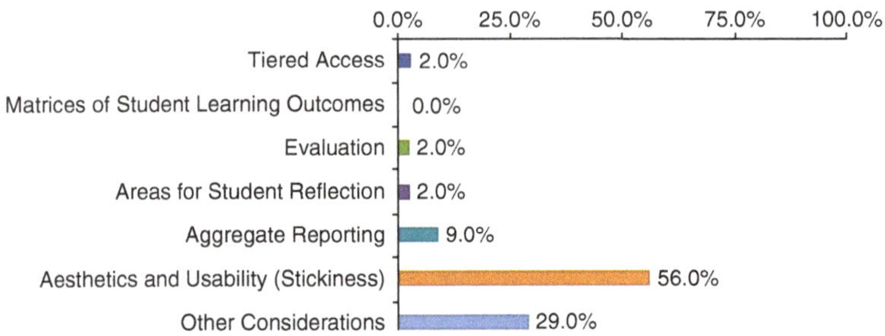

Fig. 10.2 Student perspective ePortfolio selection criteria weights

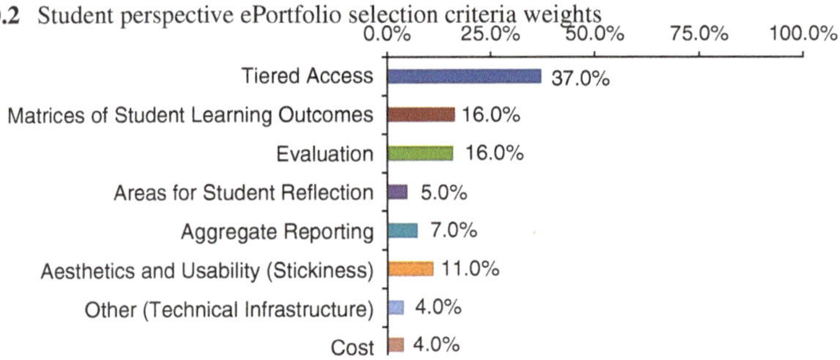

Fig. 10.3 Administrator lperspective ePortfolio selection criteria weights

the importance of these characteristics from each of their perspectives. For each perspective, the judgments of the different individual respondents were aggregated using the geometric mean to obtain the weights shown in Figs. 10.1—Faculty, 10.2—Students, and 10.3—Administrators. The aggregate perspective of each group of stakeholders was kept separate for analysis purposes. Notice, for example, that students and faculty give a lot of importance to the ePortfolio Aesthetics and Usability (Figs. 10.1 and 10.2) while Tiered Access—i.e., the ability of allowing access selectively (critical for accreditation purposes)—is given the greatest importance by the administrators (Fig. 10.3). Each of these hierarchies was used by the corresponding group of stakeholders to evaluate the different ePortfolio technical alternatives under consideration. The available alternatives (shown in Table 10.1) were prioritized differently depending on the specific perspective. For example,

Table 10.1 Integration of the priorities of different alternatives from the faculty, students, and administrators' perspectives

	Faculty (F)	Students (S)	Admin (A)	Geometric mean (GM) ($F * S * A$)	Normalized results GM/GM_SUM
Foliotek©	(1) 0.80	(1) 0.83	(1) 0.80	0.8099	(1) 0.80
LiveText©	(2) 0.64	(2) 0.66	(2) 0.64	0.6466	(2) 0.64
Epsilen©	(3) 0.61	(3) 0.70	(3) 0.60	0.6351	(3) 0.60
iWebfolio™	(4) 0.58	(4) 0.59	(4) 0.60	0.5899	(4) 0.60
GM_SUM				2.6815	

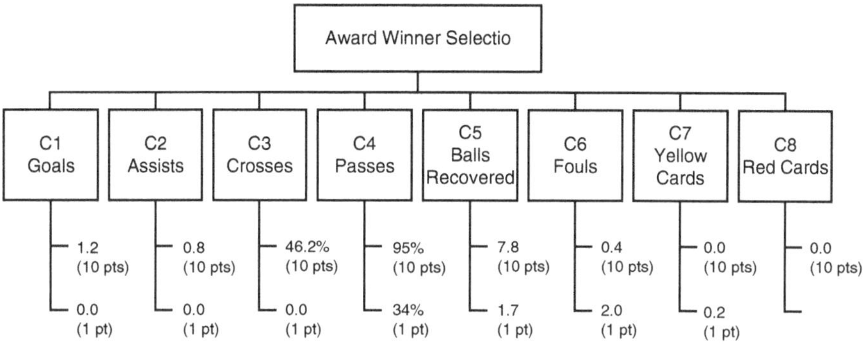

Fig. 10.4 AHP model selection of the golden ball winner

Foliotek© was ranked as #1 by the faculty (priority: 0.80), students (priority: 0.83), and administration (priority: 0.80). The priorities of the different alternatives, as reported by each group of stakeholders, were integrated using a geometric mean. For example, for the *Foliotek*© alternative, the integrated result is obtained by first multiplying the three different results (0.80 * 0.83 * 0.80) and next obtaining its cubic root as shown in Table. 10.1.

The advantage of using an AHP approach to evaluate the ePortfolio alternatives is that the different hierarchies allow us to understand the different perspectives and to make the negotiation process much easier. When we understand the point of view of the other party, we can understand its rationality rather than attributing it simply to stubbornness, and make us more willing to look for common ground.

10.2 AHP Ratings Model in Public Decisions

One of the most popular uses of ratings model is for the evaluation of candidates to obtain a winner. A simple application to assess the winner of the FIFA'S Golden Ball in the 2014 Soccer World Cup is reported by Mu (2014) and shown in Fig. 10.4.

In this application, the highest performance obtained by the players constituted the maximum score of 10 points while the lowest performance corresponded to 0 points. For example, for C1-Goals criterion, the greatest ratio of goals per game was 1.2; therefore, this performance constituted 10 points. The lowest goal ratio had been 0 goals per game; therefore, 0 goals/game constituted the lowest possible score of 1 point.[1] Similarly, in the case of successful pass ratios, the highest performance ratio was 95%; therefore, this constituted the maximum score of 10 points while the lowest pass success ratio was 34%; therefore, this constituted the lowest possible score of 1 point. In the case of negative behaviors such as fouls, the lower the number of fouls the higher the score and vice versa. The only exception was in the case of C8—Red Cards since none of the candidates to the golden ball had ever gotten a red card (expulsion from the game); therefore, all candidates would be rated with the highest possible score (10 points) in this category.

The advantage of using a ratings model to evaluate award winners has the advantage of making the decision fully transparent. In public decision-making, the most important element for managerial trust is given by the transparency in the decision-making process. We may not agree with a specific decision but we certainly understand how the decision was made.

10.3 Use of AHP to Elicit Tacit Knowledge

Nonaka and Takeushi (1995) classified knowledge into explicit and tacit. Explicit knowledge can be explained, coded, packaged, and easily transmitted from one person to the other. For example, when these authors are ready to submit a paper to a journal, we rely on the "Author's Guidelines" that provide instructions about the paper format, page length, etc. This constitutes explicit knowledge. On the other hand, when a chef explains how to cook a specific dish, a recipe can provide the explicit knowledge in part but the tacit knowledge (what we would call the tricks based on the chef's experience) is usually left out. This may occur simply because the person is unaware of this tacit knowledge or does not know how to explain it.

Several validation studies have been conducted over the years to illustrate the effectiveness of the AHP to facilitate the eliciting of tacit knowledge in the decision-making process. In one classic validation study (Saaty, 2008; Whitaker, 2007), a group of participants were shown the geometric figures in Fig. 10.5 and were requested to rank the geometric figures in terms of area size and to estimate the relative areas of each figure (e.g., the participant may guess that geometric figure A—the circle—has an area which is 30% (0.3) of the total (A + B + C + D + E) area, followed by geometric figure C—the square—which has only 20% (0.2) of the total area and so forth).

From an AHP point of view, such tasks can be conceptualized as a hierarchical decision-making task comprising a decision goal (i.e., prioritization in terms of

[1]The reader may wonder why we did not use 0 as the lowest possible score. While the range of points for the rating scale is arbitrary, we decided to have a scale from 1 to 10 simply because in several criteria the lowest performance did not mean lack of performance (e.g., C4—successful passes). However, as previously indicated the scale itself is arbitrary.

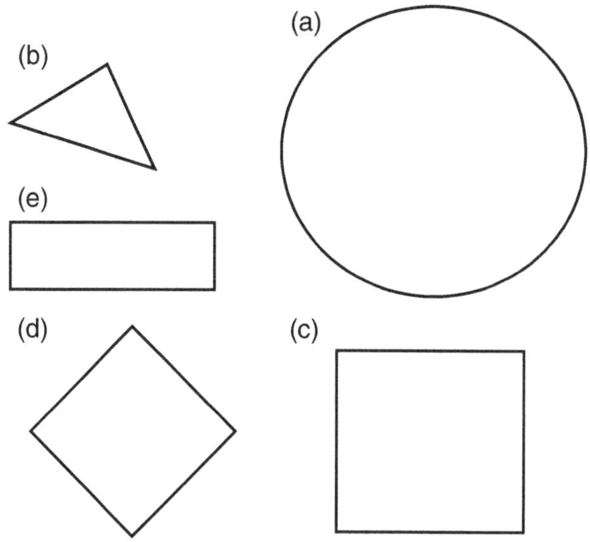

Fig. 10.5 Geometric figures task: estimating relative areas of geometric figures

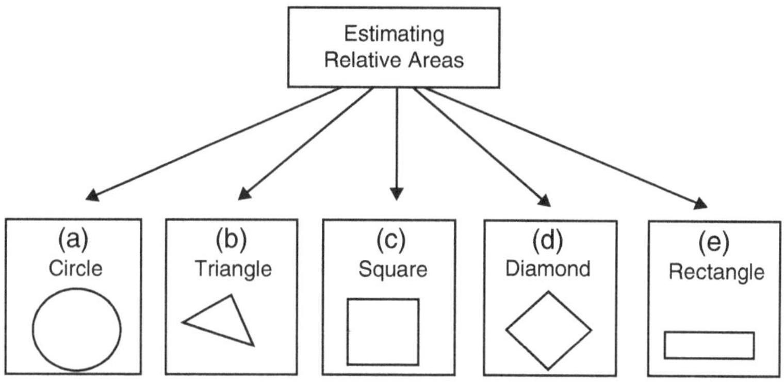

Fig. 10.6 Prioritization of relative areas based on the AHP methodology

areas) and the alternatives to choose from (i.e., the different geometric figures), as shown in Fig. 10.6.

In technical terms, the AHP method consists of pairwise comparisons of the areas of the geometric figures followed by a calculation of the final priorities. Both the pairwise comparisons and the final relative areas obtained (constituted by the priorities) are shown in Table 10.2. When the final relative priorities (areas) are compared against the actual relative sizes, we can see that the differences are minimal (compare the Priorities column with the actual relative sizes in Table 10.2).

Similar validation studies have been conducted using problems with known answers ranging from estimating the amount of drinks consumed in the USA to the relative weights of different objects (Whitaker, 2007). In all cases, the AHP meth-

Table 10.2 Completed pairwise comparison matrix for the geometric figures task (Saaty 2008)

Alternatives	A (circle)	B (triangle)	C (square)	D (diamond)	E (rectangle)	Priorities (eigenvector)	Actual relative sizes
A—circle	1	9	2	3	5	0.462	0.471
B—triangle	1/9	1	1/5	1/3	1/2	0.049	0.050
C—square	1/2	5	1	3/2	3	0.245	0.234
D—diamond	1/3	3	2/3	1	3/2	0.151	0.149
E—rectangle	1/5	2	1/3	2/3	1	0.093	0.096

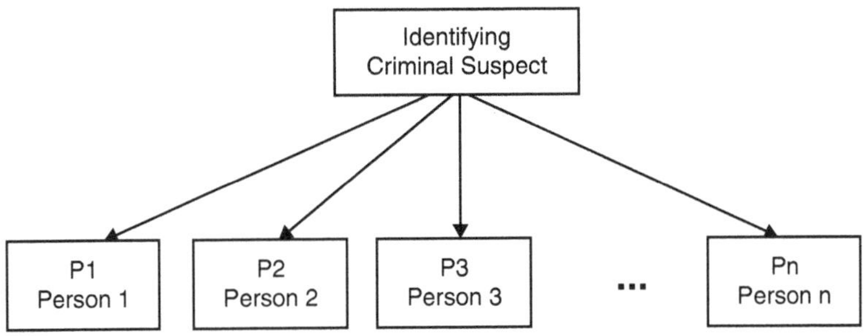

Fig. 10.7 Eyewitness identification as an AHP decision-making process

odology enables the decision-maker to develop priorities that are very close to the actual values. In other words, AHP is an effective tool for optimizing the outcome quality of complex decisions.

Based on the above rationale, Mu and Chung (2013) have proposed the use of AHP for the identification of criminal suspects. Eyewitness identification or the process of selecting a criminal suspect out of a lineup of potential candidates can be modeled as a complex decision-making problem that involves the prioritization of the candidates, as illustrated in Fig. 10.7. Applying the AHP methodology not only provides a structured approach to eyewitness identification, it also allows quantification of the quality of the identification in more nuanced ways.

Applying the AHP methodology to the eyewitness identification procedure entails two significant departures from the current paradigm. First, the AHP methodology requires the presentation of potential suspects in a pairwise (PAIR) fashion. Second, with each pair of suspects, the eyewitness would form a relative judgment on a ratio scale (i.e., between 1 and 9) with respect to the person recalled from memory. This is qualitatively distinct from the categorical format (i.e., Yes or No) of eyewitness responses in the current method of sequential (SEQ) lineup.

Given the track record of AHP in optimizing decision quality, it has been proposed that the PAIR presentation format would increase the rate of correct identifications and lower the rate of incorrect identifications. In other words, the following hypotheses have been proposed:

H1:	The rate of correct identifications is greater with the PAIR lineup than in SEQ lineup
H2:	The rate of incorrect identifications is lower with the PAIR lineup than either SEQ lineups

The preliminary study of Mu and Chung (2013) supports the above hypothesis. Furthermore, follow-up studies also suggest that the AHP approach advantage can be extended to lineups in which the criminal is absent from the lineup (Mu et al., 2015). Still, more studies are being performed by this research team.

10.4 Conclusion

The purpose of this chapter is to provide some additional examples of the use of AHP in different decision settings and emphasizing the advantages obtained by doing so. However, the reader must have noticed at this point that working with AHP is rather similar to working with LEGO blocks. The number of different blocks is rather limited and relatively easy to grasp; however, the possibilities of what can be done with them is rather unlimited. Similarly, using a relative limited set of concepts: hierarchical modeling, pairwise comparison, consistency, synthesis, and sensitivity; it is possible to address a very broad number of decision-making problems and situations.

References

Mu, E. (2014). An MCDM reflection on the FIFA 2014 world cup golden ball award. *The International Journal of the Analytic Hierarchy Process, 6*(2), 124–131.

Mu, E., & Chung R. (2013). A new approach to eyewitness police identification. *Proceedings of the international symposium of the analytic hierarchy process (ISAHP)*. Malaysia, 23–26 June.

Mu, E., Wormer, S., Barkon, B., Foizey, R., & Vehec, M. (2012). Group modelling and integration of multiple perspectives in the functional selection of a new technology: The case of a next-generation electronic portfolio system. *Journal of Multi-Criteria Decision Analysis, 19*, 15–31.

Mu, E., Chung, R., & Reed, L. (2015). *New developments in using an AHP approach for eyewitness identification*. Philadelphia: INFORMS.

Nonaka, I., & Takeushi, H. (1995). *The knowledge-creating company: How Japanese companies create the dynamics of innovation* (1st ed.). New York: Oxford University Press.

Saaty, T. L. (2008). Relative measurement and its generalization in decision making why pairwise comparisons are central in mathematics for the measurement of intangible factors the analytic hierarchy/network process. *RACSAM, 102*(2), 251–318. https://doi.org/10.1007/BF03191825.

Whitaker, R. (2007). Validation examples of the analytic hierarchy process and analytic network process. *Mathematical and Computer Modelling, 46*(7–8), 840–859. https://doi.org/10.1016/j.mcm.2007.03.018.

Appendix A

Practical Questions Related to AHP Modeling

1. What is the best kind of decision problems for AHP?

While AHP can be used in a wide number of decision-making problems, AHP is traditionally used in selection, prioritization, and forecasting. AHP assumes that the decision-makers know or will come up with, individually or collectively, implicitly or explicitly, the criteria or objectives and alternatives associated with the decision. AHP is also particularly useful for situations in which we have both tangible and intangible criteria to consider in the decision.

2. How many hierarchies are needed to perform AHP Analysis?

When working with a single type of stakeholder, one hierarchy may be enough (or 4 if you perform a BOCR analysis); however, when working with different types of stakeholders, a hierarchy for each perspective may be needed. In any case, there are no rules about the number of hierarchies to analyze a problem.

3. How many criteria are needed for the AHP hierarchy?

Saaty's scale intensity, as well as AHP as a whole, is based on the findings from cognitive science that suggest that a person's working memory capacity is in the order of 7 ± 2, that is between 5 and 9 elements. This suggests that 5–9 criteria should be the ideal. If you have more than that, you may consider grouping some of them into an overall criterion and creating sub-criteria for it (e.g., cost can group sub-criteria such as acquisition cost and maintenance cost). An important step in the process, which is not usually properly addressed, is the importance of modeling the problem with a correct hierarchy. If the criteria are incomplete or they are not clearly defined and different from each other, the model will not be a good fit for the decision at hand and any decision obtained this way will be sub par.

4. How many levels should an AHP hierarchy have?

The same rationale from the previous question can be applied here. While there is not a limit to the number of levels in a hierarchy, you may want to keep it within the 7 ± 2 limit, if possible. One way to do this is by decomposing the problem into a set of hierarchies rather than using a big gigantic hierarchy.

5. Does AHP eliminate cognitive bias problems?

While cognitive biases may certainly affect the judgments we make when comparing elements in the model, the visibility and transparency of the decision-making

E. Mu, M. Pereyra-Rojas, *Practical Decision Making using Super Decisions v3*, SpringerBriefs in Operations Research, https://doi.org/10.1007/978-3-319-68369-0

process allows us to detect potential biases much more easily, in particular during the sensitivity analysis.

6. In a nutshell, what are the advantages of using AHP?

In terms of advantages, the most important ones are: (a) the ability of structuring a problem in a way that is easily manageable, (b) making the decision criteria explicit and the decision-making process transparent as a whole, (c) deriving priorities through a rigorous mathematical process using ratio scales, (d) allowing measuring and comparison of tangible and intangible elements, and (e) allowing easy sharing of the decision-making process for feedback and buy-in.

7. What are the potential limitations of using AHP?

Based on our experience in the use of AHP, the following limitations have been found: (a) the comparison process may be long if the decision is complex, (b) the comparison judgment may be unreliable if the participants are not fully engaged in the process, (c) the decision-making transparency may be counterproductive for managers who are interested in manipulating the results, and (d) group decision-making may make difficult to handle consistency problems.

Appendix B

Fig. B.1 Basic AHP model example

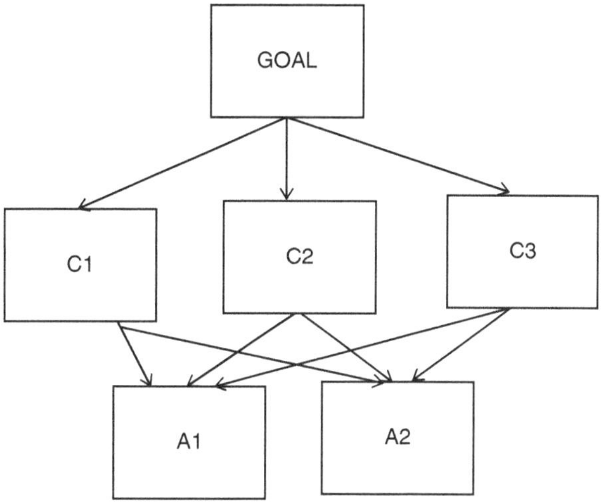

AHP Basic Theory

We present here, for the purpose of completeness, the basics of the AHP theory.[1] While the theoretical fundamentals were presented by Saaty (2012), Brunnelli (2015) and Ishizaka and Nemery (2013) also do a good job of presenting the AHP theoretical fundamentals in a very accessible way. AHP methodology requires the following steps: first, development of the hierarchy (goal, criteria, and alternatives); second, assessing relative weights of the criteria; third, assessing the alternatives relative priority with respect to criteria and finally, calculating the overall priorities. These steps will be explained with a simple model (Fig. B.1).

[1]This appendix is optional and some basic knowledge of linear algebra and vector notation is required.

E. Mu, M. Pereyra-Rojas, *Practical Decision Making using Super Decisions v3*, SpringerBriefs in Operations Research, https://doi.org/10.1007/978-3-319-68369-0

Relative Intensity	Importance	Explanation
1	Equal	Both criteria are equally important
3	Moderately	One criterion is moderately more important than the other
5	Strong	One criterion is strongly more important than the other
7	Very Strong	One criterion is very strongly more important than the other
9	Extreme	One criterion is extremely more important than the other
2,4,6,8	Intermediate Values	Compromise is needed

Fig. B.2 Intensity scale for criteria pairwise comparison.

Fig. B.3 Pairwise comparison matrix.

	C1	C2	C3	Weights
C1	1	1/5	1	0.481
C2	5	1	1/3	0.114
C3	1	3	1	0.405

Development of the Hierarchy

In a basic AHP hierarchy, we may consider three levels (as shown in Fig. B.1): the goal, the criteria,[2] and the alternatives.

Assessing Criteria Relative Importance

In the AHP example shown in Fig. B.1, the C_1–C_3 criteria are used to evaluate the alternatives. However, not all the criteria have the same importance for the decision-makers. It could be that for one institution C_3 has greater importance than C_2. In AHP, the criteria need to be compared pairwise with respect to the goal to establish their relative importance using an intensity scale developed for this purpose as shown in Fig. B.2.

Using the scale from Fig. B.2, we will ask questions such as: With respect to the purpose of this decision, which is more important criterion "C_3" or "C_2"? If we consider that C_3 is moderately more important than C_2, we are mathematically stating $C_3/C_2 = 3$ (using the scale from Fig. B.3). Notice that this judgment automatically

[2] In more complex hierarchies, the criteria may have sub-criteria and it is also possible that alternatives may have sub-alternatives.

implies that the comparison of C_2 with C_3 will yield the ratio $C_2/C_3 = 1/3$. This constitutes the reciprocity rule that can be expressed mathematically as $C_{ij} = 1/C_{ji}$ where i and j are any element (i corresponds to the row and j refers to the column) in the comparison matrix.

These judgments are recorded in a comparison matrix as shown in Fig. B.3. Notice that the judgment diagonal, given that the importance of a criterion compared with itself (C_{ij}/C_{ij}), will always be equal and is 1 in the comparison matrix. Also, only the comparisons that fill in the upper part of the matrix (shaded area) are needed. The judgments in the lower part of the comparison matrix are the reciprocals of the values in the upper part, as shown in Fig. B.3.

Another important consideration when completing the comparison matrix is the extent to which it respects the transitivity rule. If the importance of $C_1/C_2 = 1/5$, and the importance of $C_2/C_3 = 1/3$, then it is expected that $C_1/C_3 = (1/5) \times (1/3) = 1/15$. In other words, $C_{ij} = C_{ik} \times C_{kj}$ where C_{ij} is the comparison of criteria i and j. However, this is not the case in Fig. B.3 where $C_1/C_3 = 1$ as indicated by the decision-maker. This means there is some inconsistency in this matrix of judgment as will be explained next.

Checking Consistency of Judgments

Any comparison matrix that fulfills the reciprocity and transitivity rules is said to be consistent. The reciprocity rule is relatively easy to respect, whenever you elicit the judgment C_{ij} you make a point of recording the judgment C_{ji} as the reciprocal value in the comparison. However, it is much harder to comply with the transitivity rule because of the use of English language verbal comparisons from Fig. B.2 such as "strongly more important than," "very strongly more important than," "extremely more important than," and so forth.

Deriving criteria weights in AHP only makes sense if the comparison matrix is consistent or near consistent, and to assess this Saaty (2012) has proposed a consistency index (CI) as follows:

$$\mathrm{CI} = (\lambda_{\max} - \mathrm{N}) / (\mathrm{N} - 1)$$

where $\lambda_{\max}$ is the matrix maximal eigenvalue. This is used to calculate the consistency ratio defined as:

$$\mathrm{CR} = \mathrm{CI} / \mathrm{RI}$$

where RI is the random index (the average CI of 500 randomly filled matrices which is available in published tables). CR less than 10% means that the inconsistency is less than 10% of 500 random matrices. CR values of 0.1 or below constitute acceptable consistency.

$$\mathrm{CR} = 0.028$$

For the comparison matrix used in our example analysis, CR can be calculated as being 0.028, which constitutes an acceptable consistency and means that we can proceed to calculate the priorities (weights) for our criteria comparison matrix shown in Fig. B.3.[3]

[3] Given the extensive availability of commercial (e.g., Decision Lens, Expert Choice) and freely available software (e.g., Super Decisions, MakeItRational), we do not show the calculations here

Deriving Criteria Weights

The vector of priorities (or weights) **p** for the criteria matrix, given that it is consistent, is calculated by solving the equation (Ishizaka & Nemery, 2013):

$$\mathbf{Cp} = \mathrm{n}\mathbf{p}$$

where n is the matrix dimension of **C**, the criteria matrix, and $\mathbf{p} = (p_1, p_2, \ldots p_n)$.

Saaty (2012) demonstrated that for a consistent matrix, the priority vector is obtained by solving the equation above. However, for an inconsistent matrix, this equation is no longer valid. Therefore, the dimension n is replaced by the unknown λ. The calculation of λ and p is constituted by solving the eigenvalue problem $\mathbf{Cp} = \lambda\mathbf{p}$. Any value λ satisfying this equation is called an eigenvalue and **p** is its associated eigenvector. Based on Perron theory, a positive matrix has a unique positive eigenvalue called the maximum eigenvalue $\lambda_{\max}$. For perfectly consistent matrices, $\lambda_{\max} = n$; otherwise the difference $\lambda_{\max} - n$ is a measure of the inconsistency. Software packages[4] calculate the eigenvector[5] associated to the maximum eigenvalue by elevating the comparison matrix to successive powers until the limit matrix, where all the columns are equal, is reached. Any column constitutes the desired eigenvector. The calculated priorities, using this eigenvalue method, for our tentative criteria comparison matrix are shown in the rightmost column (under the heading *Weights*) in Fig. B.3.

but simply report the consistency reported by the software package.

[4] In our applications, the open software Super Decisions was used to perform the comparison matrix calculations to obtain the eigenvector (criteria and sub-criteria weights) as well as ensuring that CR was less or equal 0.1 (SuperDecisions 2014).

[5] Naturally, there is the question if the eigenvalue is still valid for inconsistent matrices. Saaty (2012) justified this using perturbation theory which says that slight variations in a consistent matrix imply only slight variations of the eigenvector and eigenvalue (Ishizaka & Nemery 2013).

References

Brunnelli, M. (2015). *Introduction to the analytic hierarchy process*. Heidelberg: Springer.
Ishizaka, A., & Nemery, P. (2013). *Multi-criteria decision analysis: Methods and software*. West Sussex: Wiley.
Saaty, T. L. (2012). *Decision making for leaders: The analytic hierarchy process for decisions in a complex world* (3rd Rev. ed.). Pittsburgh: RWS Publications.

Index

E. Mu, M. Pereyra-Rojas, *Practical Decision Making using Super Decisions v3*, SpringerBriefs in Operations Research, https://doi.org/10.1007/978-3-319-68369-0

Kolibri 360 GmbH
Ferdinand-Jühlke-Straße 7
99095 Erfurt, Deutschland
produktsicherheit@kolibri360.de